A Dissertation on Slavery

A
DISSERTATION
ON
SLAVERY:
WITH
A PROPOSAL
FOR THE
GRADUAL ABOLITION OF IT,
IN THE
STATE OF VIRGINIA.

By ST. GEORGE TUCKER,

PROFESSOR OF LAW IN THE UNIVERSITY OF WILLIAM
AND MARY, AND ONE OF THE JUDGES OF THE
GENERAL COURT, IN VIRGINIA.

*Slavery not only violates the Laws of Nature, and of civil
Society, it also wounds the best Forms of Government: in a
Democracy, where all Men are equal, Slavery is contrary
to the Spirit of the Constitution.* MONTESQUIEU.

PHILADELPHIA:
PRINTED FOR MATHEW CAREY,
No. 118, MARKET-STREET.

1796.

TO THE

General Assembly of Virginia,

To whom it belongs to decide upon
the expediency and practicability of a
plan for the *gradual abolition* of *Slavery*
in this commonwealth,

The following pages are most respect-
fully submitted and inscribed,

BY THE AUTHOR.

*Williamsburg, in
Virginia,* May 20, 1796.

TO THE READER.

The following pages form a part of a course of Lectures on Law and Police, delivered in the University of William and Mary, in this commonwealth. The Author considering the Abolition of Slavery in this State, as an object of the first importance, not only to our moral character and domestic peace, but even to our political salvation; and being persuaded that the accomplishment of so momentous and desirable an undertaking will in great measure depend upon the early adoption of some plan for that purpose, with diffidence submits to the consideration of his countrymen his ideas on a subject of such consequence. He flatters himself that the plan he ventures to suggest, is liable to fewer objections than most others that have been submitted to the consideration of the public, as it will be attended with a gradual change of condition in the blacks, and cannot possibly affect the interest either of creditors, or any other description of persons of the present generation: and posterity he makes no doubt will feel themselves relieved from a perilous and grievous burden by the timely adoption of a plan, whose operation may be felt by them, before they are borne down by a weight which threatens destruction to our happiness both public and private.

☞ The following ADDITIONAL NOTES have been received from the Author since the body of this work was printed off.

In page 20, *after the word* arms, *in line* 5, *read this note :*

This was the case under the laws of the state; but the Act of 2. Cong. c. 33. for establishing an uniform militia throughout the United States, seems to have excluded all but free white men from bearing arms in the militia.

To the word slave, *page* 47, *line* 14, *add the following note :*

It may not be improper here to note, that the first congress of the United States, at their third session, Dec., 1793, passed an act to prohibit the carrying on the slave trade from the United States to any foreign place or country ; the provisions of which seem well calculated to restrain the citizens of united America from embarking in so infamous a traffick.

STATE OF SLAVERY IN VIRGINIA.

IN the preceding Enquiry (a) into the absolute rights of the citizens of united America, we must not be understood as if those rights were equally and universally the privilege of all the inhabitants of the United States, or even of all those, who may challenge this land of freedom as their native country. Among the blessings which the Almighty hath showered down on these states, there is a large portion of the bitterest draught that ever flowed from the cup of affliction. Whilst America hath been the land of promise to Europeans, and their descendants, it hath been the vale of death to millions of the wretched sons of Africa. The genial light of liberty, which hath here shone with un-rivalled lustre on the former, hath yielded no comfort to the latter, but to them hath proved a pillar of darkness, whilst it hath

(a) The subject of a preceding Lecture, with which the present was immediately connected, was, An Enquiry into the Rights of Persons, as Citizens of the United States of America.

conducted the former to the most enviable
state of human existence. Whilst we were
offering up vows at the shrine of Liberty,
and sacrificing hecatombs upon her altars ;
whilst we swore irreconcilable hostility to
her enemies, and hurled defiance in their
faces ; whilst we adjured the God of Hosts
to witness our resolution to live free, or
die, and imprecated curses on their heads
who refused to unite with us in establishing
the empire of freedom ; we were imposing
upon our fellow men, who differ in complexion from us; a *flavery*, ten thousand
times more cruel than the utmost extremity of those grievances and oppressions,
of which we complained. Such are the
inconsistencies of human nature ; such the
blindness of those who pluck not the beam
out of their own eyes, whilst they can espy
a moat, in the eyes of their brother ;
such that partial system of morality which
confines rights and injuries, to particular
complexions ; such the effect of that self-
love which justifies, or condemns, not according to principle, but to the agent.
Had we turned our eyes inwardly when
we supplicated the Father of Mercies to
aid the injured and oppressed ; when we
invoked the Author of Righteousness to
attest the purity of our motives, and the

justice of our cause; *(b)* and implored the God of Battles to aid our exertions in its defence, should we not have stood more self convicted than the contrite publican? Should we not have left our gift upon the altar, that we might be first reconciled to our brethren whom we held in bondage? Should we not have loosed their chains, and broken their fetters? Or if the difficulties and dangers of such an experiment prohibited the attempt during the convulsions of a revolution, is it not our duty to embrace the first moment of constitutional health and vigour, to effectuate so desirable an object, and to remove from us a stigma, with which our enemies will never fail to upbraid us, nor our consciences to reproach us? To form a just estimate of this obligation, to demonstrate the incompatability of a state of slavery with the principles of our government, and of that revolution upon which it is founded, and to elucidate the practicability of its total, though gradual, abolition, it will be proper to consider the nature of slavery, its properties, attendants, and consequences in general; its rise, progress, and present

(b) The American standard, at the commencement of those hostilities which terminated in the revolution, had these words upon it—AN APPEAL TO HEAVEN!

state not only in this commonwealth, but in such of our sister states as have either perfected, or commenced the great work of its extirpation; with the means they have adopted to effect it, and those which the circumstances and situation of our country may render it most expedient for us to pursue, for the attainment of the same noble and important end. *(c)*

According to Justinian, * the first gene-ral division of persons, in respect to their rights, is into freemen and slaves. It is equally the glory and the happiness of that country from which the citizens of the United States derive their origin, that the traces of slavery, such as at present exists in several of the United States, are there utterly extinguished. It is not my design to enter into a minute enquiry whether it ever had existence there, nor to compare the situation of villeins, during the exist-ence of pure villenage, with that of mo-dern domestic slaves. The records of those times, at least, such as have reached this

* Lib. 1.
Tit. 2.

(c) The Author here takes the liberty of making his acknowledgments to the reverend Jeremiah Belknap, D. D. of Boston, and to Zephaniah Swift, Esq. re-presentative in congress from Connecticut, for their ob-liging communications ; he hath occasionally made use of them in several parts of this Lecture, where he may have omitted referring to them.

quarter of the globe, are too few to throw
a satisfactory light on the subject. Suffice
it that our ancestors migrating hither
brought not with them any prototype of
that slavery which hath been established
among us. — The first introduction of it
into Virginia was by the arrival of a Dutch
ship from the coast of Africa having *twenty*
Negroes on board, who were sold here in
the year 1620. * In the year 1638 we find * Stith.
them in Maſſachuſetts. *(d)* They were 182. *(d. *
introduced into Connecticut ſoon after the
ſettlement of that colony; that is to ſay,
about the ſame period. *(e).* Thus early
had our forefathers ſown the ſeeds of an
evil, which, like a leproſy, hath deſcended
upon their poſterity with accumulated ran-
cour, viſiting the ſins of the fathers upon
ſucceeding generations. — The climate of
the northern ſtates leſs favourable to the
conſtitution of the natives of Africa, † † Dr. Bel-
than the ſouthern, proved alike unfavour- knap.
able to their propagation, and to the in- Swift.
creaſe of their numbers by importations.
As the ſouthern colonies advanced in population, not only importations increaſed
there, but Nature herſelf, under a climate
more congenial to the African conſtitution,

(d) Dr. Belknap's anſwers to St. G. T.'s queries.
(e) Letter from Zephaniah Swift to St. G. T.

assisted in multiplying the blacks in those parts, no less than in diminishing their numbers, in the more rigorous climates of the north ; this influence of climate more-over contributed extremely to increase or diminish the value of the slave to the pur-chasers, in the different colonies. White labourers, whose constitutions were better adapted to the severe winters of the New England colonies, were there found to be preferable to the Negroes, * who, accus-tomed to the influence of an ardent sun, became almost torpid in those countries, not less adapted to give vigour to their laborious exercises, than unfavourable to the multiplication of their species ; in those colonies, where the winters were not only milder, and of shorter duration, but succeeded by an intense summer heat, as invigorating to the African, as debili-tating to the European constitution, the Negroes were not barely more capable of performing labour than the Europeans, or their descendants, but the multiplication of the species was at least equal ; and, where they met with humane treatment, perhaps greater than among the whites. The purchaser therefore calculated not upon the value of the labour of his slave only, but, if a female, he regarded her

*Dr. Bel-knap. Zephan. Swift.

as " the fruitful mother of an hundred more:" and many of thefe unfortunate people have there been in this ftate, whofe defcendants even in the compafs of two or three generations have gone near to realize the calculation.—The great in-creafe of flavery in the fouthern, in pro-portion to the northern ftates in the union, is therefore not attributable, *folely*, to the effect of fentiment, but to natural caufes; as well as thofe confiderations of profit, which have, perhaps, an equal influence over the conduct of mankind in general, in whatever country, or under whatever climate their deftiny hath placed them. What elfe but confiderations of this na-ture could have influenced the merchants of the freeft nation, at that time in the world, to embark in fo nefarious a traffic, as that of the human race, attended, as the African flave trade has been, with the moft atrocious aggravations of cru-elty, perfidy, and intrigues, the objects of which have been the perpetual fomen-tation of predatory and inteftine wars? What, but fimilar confiderations, could prevail on the government of the fame country, even in thefe days, to patronize a commerce fo diametrically oppofite to the generally received maxims of that government. It is to the operation of these considerations in the parent country, not less than to their influence in the colonies, that the rise, increase, and continuance of slavery in those British colonies which now constitute united America, are to be attributed, as I shall endeavour to shew in the course of the present enquiry. It is now time to enquire into the nature of slavery, in general, and take a view of its consequences, and attendants in this commonwealth, in particular.

Slavery, says a well informed writer * on the subject, has been attended with circumstances so various in different countries, as to render it difficult to give a general definition of it. Justinian calls it a constitution of the law of nations, by which one man is made subject to another, contrary to nature. † Grotius describes it to be an obligation to serve another for life, in consideration of diet, and other common necessaries. ‡ Dr. Rutherforth, rejecting this definition, informs us, that perfect slavery is an obligation to be directed by another in all one's actions. § Baron Montesquieu defines it to be the establishment of a right, which gives one man such a power over another, as renders him absolute master over his life and

* Hargrave's case of Negroe Somerset.

† Lib. 1. Tit. 3. Sect. 2.

‡ Lib. 2. c. 5. Sect. 27.

§ Lib. 1. c. 20. pa. 474.

fortune. * These definitions appear not *Lib. 15. c. 1.
to embrace the subject fully, since they
respect the condition of the slave, in regard to his *master*, only, and not in regard to the *state*, as well as the *master*.
The author last mentioned observes, that
the constitution of a state may be free,
and the subject not so. The subject free,
and not the constitution of the state. † †Lib. 12. c. 1.
Pursuing this idea, instead of attempting
a general definition of slavery; I shall,
by considering it under a threefold aspect,
endeavour to give a just idea of its nature.

I. When a nation is, from any external
cause, deprived of the right of being go-
verned by its own laws, only, such a nation may be considered as in a state of
political slavery. Such is the state of conquered countries, and generally, of colonies, and other dependant governments.
Such was the state of united America before
the revolution. In this case the personal
rights of the subject may be so far secured
by wholesome laws, as that the individual
may be esteemed free, whilst the state
is subject to a higher power: this sub-
jection of one nation, or people, to the
will of another, constitutes the first species
of slavery, which, in order to distinguish

C

it from the other two, I have called political; inasmuch as it exists only in respect to the governments, and not to the individuals of the two countries. Of this it is not our business to speak, at present.

II. Civil liberty being no other than natural liberty so far restrained by human laws, and no farther, as is necessary and expedient for the general advantage of the public,* whenever that liberty is, by the laws of the state, further restrained than is necessary and expedient for the general advantage, a state of *civil slavery* commences immediately: this may affect the whole society, and every description of persons in it, and yet the constitution of the state be perfectly free. And this happens whenever the laws of a state respect the form, or energy of the government, more than the happiness of the citizen; as in Venice, where the most oppressive species of civil slavery exists, extending to every individual in the state, from the poorest gondolier to the members of the senate, and the doge himself.

This species of slavery also exists whenever there is an inequality of rights, or privileges, between the subjects or citizens of the same state, except such as necessarily result from the exercise of a pub-

* Blackstone's Com. c. 125.

lic office ; for the pre-eminence of one clafs of men muft be founded and erected upon the depreffion of another ; and the meafure of exaltation in the former, is that of the flavery of the latter. In all governments, however conftituted, or by what defcription foever denominated, wherever the diftinction of rank prevails, or is admitted by the conftitution, this fpecies of flavery exifts. It exifted in every nation, and in every government in Europe before the French revolution. It exifted in the American colonies before they became independent ftates ; and notwithftanding the maxims of equality which have been adopted in their feveral conftitutions, it exifts in moft, if not all, of them, at this day, in the perfons of our free Negroes and mulattoes ; whofe civil incapacities are almoft as numerous as the civil rights of our free citizens. A brief enumeration of them, may not be improper before we proceed to the third head.

Free Negroes and mulattoes are by our conftitution excluded from the right of fuffrage, *(f)* and by confequence, I appre-

(f) The Conftitution of Virginia, art. 7. declares, that the right of fuffrage fhall remain as then exercifed : the act of 1723, c. 4 (edit. 1733,), fect. 23, declared, that no Negroe, mulattoe, or Indian, fhall have any

hend; from office too : they were formerly incapable of ferving in the militia, except as drummers or pioneers, but now I prefume they are enrolled in the lifts of thofe that bear arms, though formerly punifhable for prefuming to appear at a mufter-field. * During the revolution war many of them were enlifted as foldiers in the regular army. Even flaves were not rejected from military fervice at that period, and fuch as ferved faithfully during the period of their enliftment; were emancipated by an act paffed after the conclufion of the war. † An act of juftice to which they were entitled upon every principle. All but houfekeepers, and perfons refiding upon the frontiers are prohibited from keeping, or carrying any gun, powder, fhot, club, or other weapon offenfive or defenfive : ‡ Refiftance to a white perfon, in any cafe, was, formerly, and now, in any cafe, except a wanton affault on the Negroe or mulattoe, is punifhable by whipping. § No Negroe or mulattoe can be a witnefs

*1723. c. 2.

† Oct. 1783. c. 3.

‡1748. c. 31. Edit. 1794.

§ Ib. c. 103.

vote at the election of burgeffes, or any other election whatfoever.—This act, it is prefumed, was in force at the adoption of the conftitution.—The act of 1785, c. 55 (edit. of 1794, c. 17,), alfo exprefsly excludes them from the right of fuffrage.

in any profecution, or civil fuit, in which a white perfon is a party. * Free Negroes together with flaves were formerly denied the benefit of clergy in cafes where it was allowed to white perfons; but they are now upon an equal footing as to the allowance of clergy, though not as to the confequence of that allowance, inafmuch as the court may fuperadd other corporal punifhments to the burning in the hand ufually inflicted upon white perfons, in the like cafes. † Emancipated Negroes may be fold to pay the debts of their former mafter contracted before their emancipation; and they may be hired out to fatisfy their taxes where no fufficient diftrefs can be had. Their children are to be bound out apprentices by the overfeers of the poor. Free Negroes have all the advantages in capital cafes, which white men are entitled to, except a trial by a jury of their own complexion: and a flave fuing for his freedom fhall have the fame privilege. Free Negroes refiding, or employed to labour in any town muft be regiftered; the fame thing is required of fuch as go at large in any county. The penalty in both cafes is a fine upon the perfon employing, or harbouring them, and imprifonment of the

* 1794. c. 141.

† 1794. c. 103.

* 1794.
c. 163.

† 1794.
c. 164.

‡ Inft. lib.
1. tit. 1.

Negroe. * The migration of free Negroes or mulattoes to this ftate is alfo prohibited; and thofe who do migrate hither may be fent back to the place from whence they came.† Any perfon, not being a Negroe, having one-fourth or more Negroe blood in him is deemed a mulattoe. The law makes no other diftinction between Negroes and mulattoes, whether flaves or freemen. Thefe incapacities and difabilities are evidently the fruit of the third fpecies of flavery, of which it remains to fpeak; or, rather, they are fcions from the fame common ftock: which is,

III. That condition in which one man is fubject to be directed by another in all his actions; and this conftitutes a ftate of *domeftic flavery*; to which ftate all the incapacities and difabilities of civil flavery are incident, with the weight of other numerous calamities fuperadded thereto. And here it may be proper to make a fhort enquiry into the origin and foundation of domeftic flavery in other countries, previous to its fatal introduction into this.

Slaves, fays Juftinian, are either born fuch or become fo.‡ They are born flaves when they are children of bond women; and they become flaves, either

by the law of nations, that is, by captivity;
for it is the practice of our generals to
fell their captives, being accustomed to
preserve, and not to destroy them: or
by the civil law, which happens when a
free person, above the age of twenty,
suffers himself to be sold for the sake of
sharing the price given for him. The
author of the Commentaries on the Laws
of England thus combats the reasonable-
ness of all these grounds: * " The con- *1. b. c.
queror," says he, " according to the ci- 423.
" vilians, had a right to the life of his
" captives; and having spared that, has
" a right to deal with him as he pleases.
" But it is an untrue position, when taken
" generally, that by the law of nature
" or nations, a man may kill his enemy:
" he has a right to kill him only in par-
" ticular cases; in cases of absolute ne-
" cessity for self-defence; and it is plain
" that this absolute necessity did not sub-
" sist, since the victor did not actually kill
" him, but made him prisoner. War
" itself is justifiable only on principles
" of self-preservation; and therefore it
" gives no other right over prisoners but
" merely to disable them from doing
" harm to us, by confining their persons:
" much less can it give a right to kill,

" torture, abuſe, plunder, or even to
" enſlave, an enemy, when the war is ver.
" Since therefore the right of *making* ſlaves
" by captivity, depends on a ſuppoſed
" right of ſlaughter, that foundation fail-
" ing, the conſequence drawn from it
" muſt fail likewiſe. ; But, ſecondly, it
" is ſaid ſlavery, may begin *jure civili ;*
" when one man ſells himſelf to another.
" This, if only meant of contracts to
" ſerve, or work for, another, is very
" juſt: but when applied to ſtrict ſlavery,
" in the ſenſe of the laws of old Rome or
" modern Barbary, is alſo impoſſible.
" Every ſale implies a price, a *quid pro*
" *quo,* an equivalent given to the ſeller,
" in lieu of what he transfers to the
" buyer ; but what equivalent can be
" given for life and liberty, both of
" which, in abſolute ſlavery, are held
" to be in the maſter's diſpoſal ? His
" property, alſo, the very price he
" ſeems to receive, devolves, *ipſo facto,*
" to his maſter, the inſtant he becomes a
" ſlave. In this caſe, therefore, the
" buyer gives nothing, and the ſeller
" receives nothing : of what validity
" then can a ſale be, which deſtroys the
" very principles upon which all ſales
" are founded ? Laſtly we are told, that

" befides thefe two ways by which flaves
" are acquired, they may alfo be here-
" ditary; " *fervi nafcuntur ;*" the chil-
" dren of acquired flaves are, " jure na-
" turæ," by a negative kind of birthright,
" flaves alfo.—But *this, being built on the*
" *two former rights,* muft *fall* together
" with them. If neither captivity, nor
" the fale of one's felf, can by the law
" of nature and reafon reduce the parent
" to flavery, *much lefs* can they reduce
" the offspring." Thus by the moft
clear, manly, and convincing reafoning
does this excellent author refute every
claim upon which the practice of flavery
is founded, or by which it has been fuppofed to be juftified, at leaft, in modern
times. *(g)* But were we even to admit,
that a captive taken in a *juft war*, might
by his conqueror be reduced to a ftate of
flavery, this could not juftify the claim of
Europeans to reduce the natives of Africa
to that ftate: it is a melancholy, though
well-known fact, that in order to furnifh
fupplies of thefe unhappy people for the
purpofes of the flave trade, the Europeans
have conftantly, by the moft infidious (I
had almoft faid infernal) arts, fomented

(g) Thefe arguments are, in fact, borrowed from
the Spirit of Laws.

a kind of perpetual warfare among the ignorant and miserable people of Africa; and instances have not been wanting, where, by the most shameful breach of faith, they have trepanned and made slaves of the *sellers* as well as the *sold*. *(h)*

(h) "About the same time (the reign of queen "Elizabeth) a traffic in the human species, called "Negroes, was introduced into England, which is "one of the most odious and unnatural branches of "trade the sordid and avaricious mind of mortals ever "invented.—It had been carried on before this period "by Genoese traders, who bought a patent from "Charles the fifth, containing an exclusive right of "carrying Negroes from the Portuguese settlements "in Africa, to America and the West Indies; but "the English nation had not yet engaged in the ini-"quitous traffic.—One William Hawkins, an expert "English seaman, having made several voyages to the "coast of Guinea, and from thence to Brazil and the "West Indies, had acquired considerable knowledge "of the countries. At his death he left his journals "with his son, John Hawkins, in which he described "the lands of America and the West Indies as ex-"ceedingly rich and fertile, but utterly neglected for "want of hands to improve them. He represented "the natives of Europe as unequal to the task in such "a scorching climate; but those of Africa as well "adapted to undergo the labours requisite. Upon "which John Hawkins immediately formed a design "of transporting Africans into the western world; "and having drawn a plan for the execution of it, he "laid it before some of his opulent neighbours for

That such horrid practices have been
sanctioned by a civilized nation ; that a

" encouragement and approbation. To them it ap-
" peared promising and advantageous. A subscription
" was opened and speedily filled up, by Sir Lionel
" Ducket, Sir Thomas Lodge, Sir William Winter,
" and others, who plainly perceived the vast profits
" that would result from such a trade. Accordingly
" three ships were fitted out, and manned by an hun-
" dred select sailors, whom Hawkins encouraged to
" go with him by promises of good treatment and
" great pay. In the year 1562 he set sail for Africa,
" and in a few weeks arrived at the country called
" Sierra Leona, where he began his commerce with
" the Negroes. While he trafficked with them, he
" found the means of giving them a charming descrip-
" tion of the country to which he was bound ; the
" unsuspicious Africans listened to him with apparent
" joy and satisfaction, and seemed remarkably fond of
" his European trinkets, food, and clothes. He
" pointed out to them the barrenness of the country,
" and their naked and wretched condition, and pro-
" mised if any of them were weary of their miserable
" circumstances, and would go along with him, he
" would carry them to a plentiful land, where they
" should *live happy*, and *receive* an abundant *recompence*
" for their labours. He told them the country was
" inhabited by such men as himself and his jovial com-
" panions, and *assured* them of *kind usage* and *great*
" *friendship*. In short, the Negroes were overcome
" by his flattering promises, and *three hundred* stout
" fellows accepted his offer, and consented to embark
" along with him. Every thing being settled on the
" most amicable terms between them, Hawkins made

-nation ardent in the caufe of liberty, and
enjoying its bleffings in the fulleft extent,

" preparations for his voyage. But in the night be-
" fore his departure his Negroes were attacked by a
" large body from a different quarter; Hawkins, being
" alarmed with the fhrieks and cries of dying perfons,
" ordered his men to the affiftance of his flaves, and
" having furrounded the affailants, carried a number
" of them on board as prifoners of war. The next
" day he fet fail for Hifpaniola with his cargo of
" human creatures ; but during the paffage, he treated
" the prifoners of war in a different manner from his
" volunteers. Upon his arrival he difpofed of his cargo
" to great advantage ; and endeavoured to inculcate
" on the Spaniards who bought the negroes the fame
" diftinction to be obferved : but they having *purchafed*
" *all at the fame rate*, confidered them as flaves of the
" fame condition, and confequently treated all alike."
Hawkins having returned to England, foon after
made preparations for a fecond voyage. " In his
" paffage he fell in with the Minion man of war,
" which accompanied him to the Coaft of Africa.
" After his arrival he began as formerly to traffic with
" the Negroes, endeavouring by perfuafions and
" *profpects* of *reward*, to induce them to go along
" with him—but now they were more referved and
" jealous of his defigns, and as none of their neigh-
" bours had returned, they were apprehenfive he had
" killed and eat them The crew of the man of war
" obferving the Africans backward and fufpicious,
" began to laugh at his gentle and dilatory methods of
" proceeding, and propofed having immediate recourfe
" to force and compulfion—but Hawkins confidered
" it as cruel and unjuft, and tried by perfuafions, pro-

can continue to vindicate a right established upon such a foundation; that a peo-

" mises and threats, to prevail on them to desist from a
" purpose so unwarrantable and barbarous. In vain
" did he urge his authority and instructions from the
" Queen : the bold and headstrong sailors would hear
" of no restraints. Drunkenness and avarice are deaf
" to the voice of humanity. They pursue their violent
" design, and, after several unsuccessful attacks, in
" which *many* of them lost their *lives*, the cargo was
" at length compleated by barbarity and force.

" Hence arose that horrid and inhuman practice of
" dragging Africans into slavery, which has since been
" *so* pursued, in defiance of every principle of justice
" and religion. Had Negroes been brought from the
" flames, to which in some countries they were devoted
" on their falling prisoners of war, and in others, sacri-
" ficed at the funeral obsequies of the great and pow-
" erful among themselves ; in short had they by this
" traffic been delivered from *torture* or *death*, European
" merchants *might have some excuse* to plead in its vindi-
" cation. *But according to the common mode in which it*
" *has been conducted*, we must confess it a difficult
" matter to conceive a *single* argument in its defence.
" And though policy has given countenance and
" sanction to the trade, yet every candid and impartial
" man must confess, that it is atrocious and unjustifiable
" in every light in which it can be viewed, and turns
" merchants into a band of robbers, and trade into
" atrocious acts of fraud and violence." Historical
Account of South-Carolina and Georgia. Anonymous.
London printed in 1779—page 20, &c.

" The number of Negroe slaves bartered for in one
" year (viz. 1768), on the Coast of Africa from Cape

ple who have declared, " That *all men*
are by nature *equally* free* and *independent*," and have made this declaration
the firft article in the foundation of their
government; fhould in defiance of fo facred a truth, recognized by themfelves in
fo folemn a manner, and on fo important an
occafion, tolerate a practice incompatible
therewith, is fuch an evidence of the
weaknefs and inconfiftency of human nature, as every man who hath a fpark of
patriotic fire in his bofom muft wifh to
fee removed from his own country. If
ever there was a caufe; if ever an occafion, in which all hearts fhould be united,
every nerve ftrained, and every power
exerted, furely the reftoration of human
nature to its inalienable right is fuch:
Whatever obftacles, therefore, may hi-
therto have retarded the attempt, he that
can appreciate the honour and happinefs of his country, will think it time
that we fhould attempt to furmount
them.

But how loudly foever reafon, juftice,

" Blanco, to Rio Congo, amounted to 104,000 fouls,
" whereof more than half (viz. 53,000) were fhipped
" on account of Britifh merchants, and 6,300 on the
" account of Britifh Americans." The Law of Retribution by Granville Sharpe, Efq. page 147. note.

and; (may I not add) religion, *(i)* condemn the practice of slavery, it is acknowledged to have been very ancient, and almost universal. The Greeks, the Romans, and the ancient Germans also practised it, as well as the more ancient Jews and Egyptians. By the Germans it was tranfmitted to the various kingdoms which arofe in Europe out of the ruins of the Roman empire. In England it fubfifted for fome ages under the name of *villeinage. (k)* In Afia it feems to have

(i) See the various tracts on this fubject, by Granville Sharpe, Efq. of London.

(k) The condition of a *villein* had moft of the incidents I have before defcribed in giving the idea of *flavery*, in general. His fervices were uncertain and indeterminate, fuch as his lord thought fit to require ; or as fome of our ancient writers exprefs it, he knew not in the evening what he was to do in the morning, he was bound to do whatever he was commanded. He was liable to beating, imprifonment, and every other chaftifement his lord could devife, except killing and maiming. He was incapable of acquiring property for his own benefit ; he was himfelf the fubject of property ; as fuch faleable and tranfmiffible. If he was a villein regardant he paffed with the land to which he was annexed, but might be fevered at the will of his lord ; if he was a villein in grofs, he was an hereditament, or a chattel real, according to his lord's intereft ; being defcendible to the heir, where the lord was abfolute *owner*, and tranfmiffible to the

been general, and in Africa universal, and so remains to this day: In Europe it hath long since declined; its first declension there, is said to have been in Spain,

executor where the lord had only a term of years in him. Lastly, the slavery extended to the issue, if the father was a villein, our law deriving the condition of the child from that of the father, contrary to the Roman law, in which the rule was, *partus sequitur ventum.* Hargrave's Case of Negroe Somerset, page 26 and 27.

The same writer refers the origin of vassalage in England, principally to the wars between the British, Saxon, Danish, and Norman nations, contending for the sovereignty of that country, in opposition to the opinion of judge Fitzherbert, who supposes villeinage to have commenced at the conquest. Ib. 27, 28. And this he proves from Spelman and other antiquaries. Ib. The writ *de nativo habendo,* by which the lord was enabled to recover his villein that had absconded from him, creates a presumption that all the natives of England were at some period reduced to a state of villeinage, the word *nativus,* which signified a villein, most clearly designating the person meant thereby to be a *native:* this etymon is obvious, as well from the import of the word *nativus,* as from the history of the more remote ages of Britain. Sir Edward Coke's Etymology, " *quia plerumque nascuntur servi,*" is one of those puerile conceits, which so frequently occur in his works, and are unworthy of so great a man.

Barrington in his observations upon *magna carta,* c. 4. observes, that the villeins who held by servile tenures were considered as so many negroes on a sugar plantation; the words " *liber homo,*" in magna carta,

(83)

so early as the eighth century; and it is
alleged to have been general about the
middle of the fourteenth, and was near
expiring in the sixteenth, when the disco-
very of the American continent, and the
eastern and western coasts of Africa gave
rise to the introduction of a new species
of slavery. It took its origin from the
Portuguese, who, in order to supply the
Spaniards with persons able to sustain the
fatigue of cultivating their new possessions
in America, particularly the islands, o-
pened a trade between Africa and America
for the sale of Negroes, about the year
1508. The expedient of having slaves for

c. 14. with all deference to sir Edward Coke, who
says they mean a *free-holder*, I understand as meaning
a free man, (1) as contradistinguished from a *villein*:
for in the very next sentence the words et *villanus* alte-
rius quam noster," occur. Villeins must certainly have
been numerous at that day, to have obtained a place in
the Great Charter. It is no less an evidence that their
condition was in a state of melioration.

In Poland, at this day, the peasants seem to be in an
absolute state of slavery, or at least of villeinage, to the
nobility, who are the land-holders.

(1) Liber homo, &c. the title of *freeman* was formerly *confined* to the *nobility* and *gentry* who were de-
scended of free ancestors.—Burgh's Political Disquisi-
tions, vol. iii. p. 400, who cites Spelman's Glossary.
voc. Liber homo.

F.

labour was not long peculiar to the Spaniards, being afterwards adopted by other European colonies: * and though some attempts have been made to stop its progress in most of the United States, and several of them have the fairest prospects of success in attempting the extirpation of it, yet in others, it hath taken such deep root, as to require the most strenuous exertions to eradicate it.

The first introduction of Negroes into Virginia happened, as we have already mentioned, in the year 1620; from that period to the year 1662 there is no compilation of our laws, in print, now to be met with. In the revision made in that year, we find an act declaring that no Englishman, trader, or other, who shall bring in any Indians as servants and assign them over to any other, shall sell them for *slaves*, nor for any other time than English of like age should serve by act of assembly. † The succeeding session all children born in this country were declared to be bond, or free, according to the condition of the mother. ‡ In 1667 it was declared, " That the " conferring of baptism doth not alter the " condition of the person baptized, as to " his bondage or freedom." § This was

* Hargrave, ib.

† 1662. c. 136.

‡ 1662. Seff. d. c. 12.

§ 1667. c. 2.

done, " that divers masters freed from
" this doubt may more carefully endea-
" vour the propagating of Christianity,
" by permitting their slaves to be bap-
" tized." It would have been happy for
this unfortunate race of men if the same
tender regard for their bodies, had always
manifested itself in our laws, as is shewn
for their souls in this act. But this was
not the case ; for two years after, we
meet with an act, declaring, " That if
any slave resist his master, or others, by
his master's orders correcting him, and
by the extremity of the correction should
chance to die, such death should not be
accounted felony : but the master or other
person appointed by his master to punish
him, be acquit from molestation : *since it
could not be presumed that prepensive ma-
lice*, which alone makes *murder felony*,
should induce any man to destroy his own
estate." (l) This cruel and tyrannical

(l) Among the Israelites, according to the Mosaical
law, " If a man smote his servant, or his maid, with a
rod, and he died under his hand, he should surely be
punished—notwithstanding if he continue a day or two,
he should not be punished:' * for, saith the text, he is * Exod.
his money. Our legislators appear to have adopted the c. 21.
reason of the latter clause, without the humanity of the
former part of the law.

* 1705.
c. 49.
1723. c.
4. 1748,
c. 31.
† 1788.
c. 23.

act, was, at three different periods * re-
enacted, with very little alteration ; and
was not finally repealed till the year
1788 ;—above a century after it had first
disgraced our code. In 1668 we meet
with the first traces of emancipation, in
an act which subjects Negroe women set

‡ 1668.
c. 7.
§ 1670.
c. 5.

free to the tax on titheables. ‡ Two
years after, § an act passed prohibiting *Indians* or Negroes, manumitted, or otherwise set free, though baptized, from pur-

‖1670.
c. 12.

chasing Christian servants. ‖ From this
act it is evident that *Indians* had *before*
that time been made slaves, as well as Negroes, though we have no traces of the
original act by which they were reduced
to that condition. An act of the same
session recites that disputes had arisen
whether Indians taken in war by any other
nation, and by that nation sold to the
English, are servants for *life*, or for a
term of years ; and declaring that all *servants*, not being Christians, imported into
this country by *shipping*, shall be *slaves*
for their life-time ; but that what shall
come by land, shall serve, if boys and
girls, until thirty years of age ; if men
and women twelve years, and no longer.
On a rupture with the Indians in the year
1679 it was, for the *better encouragement*

of *soldiers*, declared that what *Indian* prisoners should be *taken in war* should be free purchase to the soldier *taking* them. * Three years after it was declared that all *servants* brought into this country by sea or land, not being Christians, whether Negroes, Moors, mulattoes or Indians, except Turks and Moors in amity with Great Britain, and all Indians which should thereafter be sold by neighbouring Indians, or any others trafficking with us, as slaves, should be slaves to all intents and purposes. † This act was re-enacted in the year 1705, and afterwards in 1753, ‡ nearly in the same terms. In 1705 an act was made, authorising a free and open trade for all persons, at all times, and at all places, with all Indians whatsoever. § On the authority of this act, the general court in April term 1787 decided that no Indians brought into Virginia since the passing thereof, nor their descendants, can be slaves in this commonwealth. (*m*)

*1679.
c. 1.

† 1682.
c. 1.
‡ 1705.
c. 49.
1753. c.
2.

§ 1705.
c. 52.

(*m*) Hannah and other Indians, against Davis.— Since this adjudication, I have met with a manuscript act of assembly made in 1691. c. 9. entitled, "An Act for a free Trade with Indians," the enacting clause of which is in the very words of the act of 1705. c. 51. A similar title to an act of that session occurs in the edition of 1733. p. 94. and the chapter is numbered as in the manuscript. If this manuscript be authentic

In October 1778 the general assembly passed the first act which occurs in our code for prohibiting the importation of slaves; * thereby declaring that no slave should thereafter be brought into this commonwealth by land, or by water; and that every slave imported contrary thereto, should upon such importation be free: with an exception as to such as might belong to persons migrating from the other states, or be claimed by descent, devise, or marriage, or be at that time the actual property of any citizen of this commonwealth, residing in any other of the United States, or belonging to travellers making a transient stay, and carrying their slaves away with them.—In 1785 this act unfortunately underwent some alteration, by declaring that slaves thereafter brought into this commonwealth, and kept therein one whole *year together*, or so long at different times as shall *amount to a year*, shall be free. By

* 1778.
c. 1.

(which there is some reason to presume, it being copied in some blank leaves at the end of Purvis's edition, and apparently written about the time of the passage of the act), it would seem that no Indians brought into Virginia for more than a century, nor any of their descendents, can be retained in slavery in this commonwealth.

this means the difficulty of proving the
right to freedom will be not a little augmented : for the fact of the first importation, where the right to freedom immediately ensued, might have been always
proved without difficulty ; but where a
slave is subject to removal from place to
place, and his right to freedom is post-
poned for so long a time as a whole year,
or perhaps several years, the provisions
in favour of liberty may be too easily
evaded. The same act declares that no
persons shall thenceforth be slaves in this
commonwealth, except such as were so
on the first day of that session (Oct. 17th,
1785), and the descendants of the females
of them. This act was re-enacted in the
revisal made in 1792. * In 1793 an addi- * See acts
tional act passed, authorising and requir- of 1794,
ing any justice of the peace having notice c. 103.
of the importation of any slaves, directly
or indirectly, from any part of Africa or
the West Indies, to cause such slave to be
immediately apprehended and transported
out of the commonwealth. † Such is the † Edit. of
rise, progress, and present foundation of 1794. c.
slavery in Virginia, so far as I have been 164.
able to trace it. The present number of
slaves in Virginia, is immense, as appears
by the census taken in 1791, amounting

to no less than 292,427 souls : nearly two-
fifths of the whole population of the commonwealth. *(n)* We may console our-
selves with the hope that this proportion

(n) Although it be true that the number of slaves
in the *whole* state bears the proportion of 292,427, to
7 7,610, the whole number of souls in the state, that
is, nearly as *two* to *five;* yet this proportion is by no
means *uniform* throughout the state. In the forty-four
counties lying upon the Bay, and the great rivers of
the state, and comprehended by a line including Bruns-
wick, Cumberland, Goochland, Hanover, Spottsylva-
nia, Stafford, Prince William and Fairfax, and the
counties eastward thereof, the number of slaves is
196,542, and the number of free persons, including
free Negroes and mulattoes, 198,371 only. So that
the blacks in that populous and extensive district of
country are *more numerous* than the whites. In the
second class, comprehending nineteen counties, and
extending from the last mentioned line to the Blue
Ridge, and including the populous counties of Frede-
rick and Berkeley, beyond the Blue Ridge, there are
82,286 slaves, and 136,251 free persons ; the number
of free persons in that class not being two to one, to
the slaves. In the third class the proportion is consi-
derably increased ; the eleven counties of which it
consists contain only 11,218 slaves, and 76,281 free
persons. This class reaches to the Allegany ridge of
mountains : the fourth and last class, comprehending
fourteen counties westward of the third class, contains
only 2,381 slaves, and 42,288 free persons. It is obvious from this statement that almost all the dangers
and inconveniences which may be apprehended from
a state of slavery on the one hand, or an attempt to

will not increase, the further importation
of slaves being prohibited, whilst the free
migrations of white people hither is encouraged. But this hope affords no other
relief from the evil of slavery, than a di-
minution of those apprehensions which
are naturally excited by the detention of
so large a number of oppressed individuals
among us, and the possibility that they
may one day be roused to an attempt to
shake off their chains.

Whatever inclination the first inhabitants of Virginia might have to encourage
slavery, a disposition to check its progress,
and increase, manifested itself in the legislature even before the close of the last
century. So long ago as the year 1669
we find the title of an act, * laying an im-   * Edit. of
position upon *servants*, and *slaves*, im-   1733. c.
ported into this country; which was ei-   12,
ther continued, revised, or increased, by
a variety of temporary acts, passed between that period and the revolution in
1776. (*o*)—One of these acts passed in
1723, by a marginal note appears to have
been repealed by proclamation, Oct. 24,

abolish it, on the other, will be confined to the people
eastward of the blue ridge of mountains.

(*o*) The following is a list of the acts, or titles of
acts, imposing duties on slaves imported, which occur

F

1724. In 1732 a duty of five per cents was laid on slaves imported, to be paid by the buyers; a measure calculated to ... in the various compilations of our laws, or in the Sessions Acts, or Journals.

render it as little obnoxious as poffible to the *English* merchants trading to Africa, and not improbably fuggefted by them, to the privy council in England. The preamble to this act is in thefe remarkable words, " We your majefty's moft duti-" ful and loyal fubjects, &c. taking into " our ferious confideration the exigencies " of your government here, and that the " duty laid upon liquors will not be fuf-" ficient to defray the neceffary expences " thereof, do humbly reprefent to your " majefty, that *no other* duty can be laid " upon our import or export, without " oppreffing your fubjects, than a duty " upon *flaves imported*, to be paid by " the buyers, *agreeable to your majefty's* " *inftructions* to your lieutenant gover-" nor." This act was only for the fhort period of four years, but feems to have been continued from time to time till the year 1751, when the duty expired, but was revived the next year. In the year 1740 an additional duty of five per cent. was impofed for four years, for the purpofe of an expedition againft the Spaniards, &c. to be likewife paid by the buyers: and in 1742 the whole duty was continued till July 1, 1747.—The act of 1752, by which thefe duties were revived and continued (as well as several former acts), takes notice that the duty had been found *no ways burdensome to the traders* in slaves. In 1754 an additional duty of five per cent. was imposed for the term of three years, by an act for encouraging and protecting the settlers on the Mississippi: this duty, like all the former, was to be paid by the buyers. · In 1759 a duty of 20 per cent. was imposed upon all slaves imported into Virginia from Maryland, North Carolina, or other places in America, to continue for seven years. In 1769 the same duty was further continued. - In the same session the duty of five per cent. was continued for three years, and an additional duty of ten per cent. to be likewise paid by the buyers, was imposed for seven years; and a further duty of five per cent. was, by a separate act of the same session, imposed for the better support of the contingent charges of government, to be paid by the buyers. In 1772 all these duties were further continued for the term of five years from the expiration of the acts then in force: the assembly at the same time petitioned the throne, *(p)*

(p) ☞ The following extract from a petition to the throne, presented from the house of burgesses of Virginia, April 1, 1772, will shew the sense of the

to remove all those restraints which inhibited his majesty's governors assenting to such laws as might check so very pernicious a commerce, as that of slavery.

people of Virginia on the subject of slavery at that period.

" The many instances of your majesty's benevolent intentions and most gracious disposition to promote the prosperity and happiness of your subjects in the colonies, encourages us to look up to the throne, and implore your majesty's paternal assistance in averting a calamity of a most alarming nature."

" The importation of slaves into the colonies from the coast of Africa hath long been considered as a trade of great inhumanity, and under its *present encouragement,* we have too much reason to fear *will endanger the very existence* of your majesty's American dominions."

" We are sensible that some of your majesty's subjects of *Great Britain* may reap emoluments from this sort of traffic, but when we consider that it greatly retards the settlement of the colonies, with *more useful* inhabitants, and may, in time, have the most destructive influence, we presume to hope that the *interest of a few* will be disregarded when placed in competition with the security and happiness of such numbers of your majesty's dutiful and loyal subjects."

Deeply impressed with these sentiments, we most humbly beseech your majesty to *remove all those restraints on your majesty's governors of this colony, which inhibit their assenting to such laws as might check so very pernicious a commerce.*" Journals of the House of Burgesses, page 131.

This petition produced no effect, as appears from

In the course of this enquiry it is easy to trace the desire of the legislature to put a stop to the further importation of slaves; and had not this desire been uniformly opposed on the part of the crown, it is highly probable that event would have taken effect at a much earlier period than it did. A duty of five per cent. to be paid by the buyers, at first, with difficulty obtained the royal assent. Requisitions from the crown for aids, on particular occasions, afforded a pretext from time to time for increasing the duty from five, to ten, and finally to twenty per cent. with which the *buyer* was uniformly made chargeable. The wishes of the people of this colony, were not sufficient to counterbalance the interest of the English merchants, trading to Africa, and it is probable, that however disposed to put a stop to so infamous a traffic by law, we should never have been able to effect it, so long as we might have continued dependant on the British government: an object sufficient of itself to justify a

the first clause of our CONSTITUTION, where among other acts of misrule, " the inhuman use of the royal negative" in refusing us permission to exclude slaves from among us by law, is enumerated, among the reasons for *separating from Great Britain.*

revolution. That the legiflature of Virginia were *fincerely* difpofed to put a ftop to it, cannot be doubted; for even during the tumult and confufion of the revolution, we have feen that they availed themfelves of the earlieft opportunity, to crufh for ever fo pernicious and infamous a commerce, by an act paffed in October 1778, the penalties of which, though apparently leffened by the act of 1792, are ftill equal to the value of the flave; being two hundred dollars upon the importer, and one hundred dollars upon every perfon buying or felling an imported flave.

A fyftem uniformly perfifted in for nearly a whole century, and finally carried into effect, fo foon as the legiflature was unreftrained by " the inhuman exercife of the royal negative," evinces the fincerity of that difpofition which the legiflature had fhewn during fo long a period, to put a check to the growing evil. From the time that the duty was raifed above five per cent. it is probable that the importation of flaves into this colony decreafed. The demand for them in the more fouthern colonies probably contributed alfo to leffen the numbers imported into this: for fome years immediately preceding the revolution, the importation of

flaves into Virginia might almoft be confidered as at an end ; and probably
would have been entirely fo, if the inge-
nuity of the merchant had not found out
the means of evading the heavy duty, by
pretended fales, at which the flaves were
bought in by fome friend, at a quarter of
their real value.

Tedious and unentertaining as this de-
tail may appear to all others, a citizen of
Virginia will feel fome fatisfaction at
reading fo clear a vindication of his country, from the opprobrium, but too la-
vifhly beftowed upon her of foftering
flavery in her bofom, whilft fhe boafts a
facred regard to the liberty of her citizens, and of mankind in general. The
acrimony of fuch cenfures muft abate, at
leaft in the breafts of the candid, upon an
impartial review of the fubject here
brought before them ; and if in addition
to what we have already advanced, they
confider the difficulties attendant on any
plan for the abolition of flavery, in a
country where fo large a proportion of the
inhabitants are flaves ; and where a ftill
larger proportion of the cultivators of the
earth are of that defcription of men, they
will probably feel emotions of fympathy
and compaffion, both for the flave and for

his master, succeed to those hasty prejudices, which even the best dispositions are
not exempt from contracting, upon subjects where there is a deficiency of information.

We are next to consider the condition
of slaves in Virginia, or the legal consequences attendant on a state of slavery in
this commonwealth; and here it is not
my intention to notice those laws, which
consider slaves, merely as *property*, and
have from time to time been enacted to
regulate the disposition of them, *as such;*
for these will be more properly considered
elsewhere: my intention at present is
therefore to take a view of such laws,
only, as regard slaves, as a distinct class
of *persons*, whose rights, if indeed they
possess any, are reduced to a much nar-
rower compass, than those, of which we
have been speaking before.

Civil rights, we may remember, are
reducible to three primary heads; the
right of personal security; the right of
personal liberty; and the right of private
property. In a state of slavery the two
last are wholly abolished, the person of
the slave being at the absolute disposal of
his master; and property, what he is incapable, in that state, either of acquiring,

G

or holding, to his own use. Hence it will appear how perfectly irreconcilable a state of slavery is to the principles of a democracy, which form the *basis* and *foundation* of our government. For our bill of rights declares, " that all men are by " nature *equally free* and independent, " and have certain rights of which they " cannot deprive or divest their posterity " —namely, the enjoyment of life and " *liberty*, with the means of *acquiring* " and *possessing property.*" This is indeed no more than a recognition of the first principles of the law of nature, which teaches us this equality, and enjoins every man, whatever advantages he may possess over another, as to the various qualities or endowments of body or mind, to practice the precepts of the law of nature to those who are in those respects his *inferiors*, no less than it enjoins his *inferiors* to practise them towards *him*. Since he has no more right to insult *them*, than they have to injure him. Nor does the *bare unkindness of nature* or of fortune condemn a man to a *worse* condition than others, as to the enjoyment of common privileges.* It would be hard to reconcile reducing the Negroes to a state of slavery to these principles, unless we first

* Spavan's Puff. vol. 1. c. 17.

degrade them below the rank of human beings, not only politically, but also physically and morally.—The Roman lawyers look upon those only properly as *persons*, who are *free*, putting *slaves* into the rank of *goods* and *chattels*; and the policy of our legislature, as well as the practice of slave-holders in America in general, seems conformable to that idea: but surely it is time we should admit the evidence of moral truth, and learn to regard them as our fellow men, and equals, except in those particulars where accident, or perhaps nature, may have given us some advantage; a recompence for which they perhaps enjoy in other respects.

Slavery, says Hargrave, always imports an obligation of perpetual service, which only the consent of the master can dissolve: it also generally gives to the master an arbitrary power of administring every sort of correction, however inhuman, not immediately affecting life or limb, and even these in some countries, as formerly in Rome, and at this day among the Asiatics and Africans, are left exposed to the arbitrary will of a master, or protected only by fines or other slight punishments. The property of the slave i, also is absolutely, the property of his master, the slave himself being the sub-ject of property, and as such saleable, or transmissible at the will of his master.—A slavery, so malignant as that described, does not leave to its wretched victims the least vestige of any civil right, and even divests them of all their natural rights. It does not, however, appear, that the rigours of slavery in this country were ever as great, as those above described: yet it must be confessed, that, at times, they have fallen very little short of them.

The first severe law respecting slaves, now to be met with in our code, is that of 1669, already mentioned, which declared that the death of a slave, *resisting his master, or other person correcting him by his order, happening by extremity of the correction*, should not be accounted felony. The alterations which this law underwent in three successive acts, *, were by no means calculated effectually to mitigate its severity ; it seems rather to have been augmented by the act of 1723, which declared that a person indicted for the murder of a slave, and found guilty of *manslaughter*, should not incur any punishment for the same. *(q)*

* 1705. c. 49. 1723, c. 4. 1748. c. 31.

(q) In December term 1788, one John Huston

All these acts were at length repealed in 1788.* So that homicide of a slave * 1788. stands now upon the same footing, as in c. 23. the case of any other person. In 1672 it was declared lawful for any person pursuing any runaway Negroe, mulattoe, Indian slave, or *servant for life*, by virtue of an *hue and cry*, to kill them in case of resistance, without being questioned for the same. † A few years afterwards this † 1672. act was extended to persons *employed to* c. 8. *apprehend* runaways. ‡ In 1705, these acts ‡ 1680. underwent some small alteration ; two c. 10. justices being authorised by proclamation to *outlaw* runaways, who might thereafter be *killed* and *destroyed* by any person whatsoever, by *such ways and means* as he may think fit, without accusation or impeachment of any crime for so doing : § § 1705. And if any such slave were apprehended, c. 49. he might be punished at the discretion of the county court, either by *dismembering*, or in any other manner *not touching life*.

was tried in the general court for the murder of a slave; the jury found him guilty of manslaughter, and the court, upon a motion in arrest of judgment, discharged him without any punishment. The general assembly being then sitting, some of the members of the court mentioned the case to some leading characters in the legislature, and the act was at the same session repealed.

The inhuman rigour of this act was afterwards * extended to the venial offence of going abroad by night, if the slave was *notoriously* guilty of it.—Such are the cruelties to which a state of slavery gives birth; such the horrors to which the human mind is capable of being reconciled, by its adoption. The dawn of humanity at length appeared in the year 1769, when the power of dismembering, even under the authority of a county court, was restricted to the single offence of *attempting* to ravish a white woman, † in which case perhaps the punishment is perhaps not more than commensurate to the crime. In 1772 some restraints were laid upon the practice of outlawing slaves, requiring that it should appear to the *satisfaction* of the justices that the slaves were outlying, and *doing mischief.* ‡ These loose expressions of the act, left too much in the discretion of men, not much addicted to weighing their import.—In 1792, every thing relative to the outlawry of slaves was *expunged* from our code, § and I trust will never again find a place in it. By the act of 1680, a Negroe, mulattoe, or Indian, bond or *free*, presuming to lift his hand in opposition to any Christian, should receive thirty lashes on his bare

* 1723.
c. 4.
1748. c.
31.

† 1769.
c. 19.

‡ 1772.
c. 9.

§ Edit.
1794. c.
103.

back for every offence. * The same act   * 1680,
prohibited slaves from carrying any club,   c. 10.
staff, gun, sword, or other weapon, of-   1705. c.
fensive or defensive. This was afterwards extended to all Negroes, mulattoes
and Indians whatsoever, with a few ex-
ceptions in favour of housekeepers, resi-
dents on a frontier plantation, and such as
were enlisted in the militia. † Slaves,   † 1723.
by these and other acts, ‡ are prohibited   c. 4.
from going abroad without leave in writ-   ‡ 1705.
ing from their masters, and if they do,   c. 49.
may be whipped: any person suffering a   1723. c.
slave to remain on his plantation for four   4. 1748.
hours together, or dealing with him with-   c. 31.
out leave in writing from his master, is   1753. c.
subject to a fine. A runaway slave may   2. 1785.
be apprehended and committed to jail,   c. 77.
and if not claimed within three months
(being first advertised) he shall be hired
out, having an iron collar first put about
his neck: and if not claimed within a
year shall be sold. § These provisions were   § 1753.
in general re-enacted in 1792, ‖ but the   c. 2.
punishment to be inflicted on a Negroe or   ‖ Edit. of
mulattoe, for lifting his hand against a   1794. c.
white person, is restricted to those cases,   103. 131.
where the former is not wantonly assault-
ed. In this act the word Indian appears
to have been designedly omitted: the

small number of these people, or their descendants remaining among us, concurring with a more liberal way of thinking, probably gave occasion to this circumstance. The act of 1748, c. 31, made it felony without benefit of clergy for a slave to prepare, exhibit, or administer any medicine whatever, without the order or consent of the master; but *allowed clergy* if it appeared that the medicine was not administered with an *ill intent ;* the act of 1792, with more justice, directs that in such case he shall be acquitted. * To consult, advise, or conspire, to rebel, or to plot, or conspire the death of any person whatsoever, is still felony without benefit of clergy in a slave. —Riots, routs, unlawful assemblies, trespasses and seditious speeches by slaves, are punishable with stripes, at the discretion of a justice of the peace. †—The master of a slave permitting him to go at large and trade as a freeman, is subject to a fine ; § and if he suffers the slave to hire himself out, the latter may be sold, and twenty-five per cent. of the price be applied to the use of the county.—Negroes and mulattoes, whether slaves or not; are incapable of being witnesses, but against, or between Negroes and mulattoes; they are not per-

* Edit.
1794. c.
103.

† 1748.
c. 31.
1794. c.
103.

‡ 1785.
c 77.
1794. c.
103.
§ 1769.
c. 19.
May
1782. c.
22. 1794.
Ib.

mitted to intermarry with any white perfon; yet no punishment is annexed to the
offence in the flave; nor is the marriage
void; but the white perfon contracting the
marriage, and the clergyman by whom it
is celebrated are liable to fine and imprifonment; and this is probably the only
inftance in which our laws will be found
more favourable to a Negroe than a white
perfon. Thefe provifions though introduced into our code at different periods,
were all re-enacted in 1792.*
*Edit. of
1794. c.
103.

From this melancholy review it will
appear that not only the right of property,
and the right of perfonal liberty, but even
the right of perfonal fecurity, has been,
at times, either wholly annihilated, or
reduced to a fhadow: and even in thefe
days, the protection of the latter feems to
be confined to very few cafes. Many actions, indifferent in themfelves, being
permitted by the law of nature to all
mankind, and by the laws of fociety to
all free perfons, are either rendered highly
criminal in a flave, or fubject him to fome
kind of punishment or reftraint. Nor is
it in this refpect only, that his condition
is rendered thus deplorable by law. The
meafure of punishment for the fame offence, is often, and the manner of trial

H

and conviction is always, different in the case of a slave, and a free-man. If the latter be accused of any crime, he is entitled to an examination before the court of the county where the offence is alleged to have been committed; whose decision, if in his favour, is held to be a legal and final acquittal; but it is not final if against him; for after this, both a grand jury, and a petit jury of the county, must successively pronounce him guilty; the former by the concurrent voices of twelve at least, of their body, and the latter, by their unanimous verdict upon oath. He may take exception to the proceedings against him, by a motion in arrest of judgment; and in this case, or if there be a special verdict, the same unanimity between his judges, as between his jurors, is necessary to his condemnation. Lastly, though the punishment which the law pronounces for his offence amount to death itself, he shall in many cases have the benefit of clergy, unless he has before received it. But in the case of a slave, the mode was formerly, and still remains essentially different. How early this distinction was adopted I have not been able to discover. The title of an act occurs, which passed in the year 1705 * for the

* 1705.
c. 11.

speedy and *easy* prosecution of slaves committing capital crimes. In 1723 * the governor was authorized, whenever any slave was committed for any capital offence, to issue a special commission of oyer and terminer, to *such persons as he should think fit,* the number being left to his discretion, who should thereupon proceed to the trial of such slave, taking for evidence the confession of the defendant, the oath of one or more credible witnesses, or such testimony of Negroes, mulattoes, or Indians, bond or free, with pregnant circumstances, as to them should seem convincing, without the solemnity of a jury. No exception, formerly, could be taken to the proceedings, on the trial of a slave,† but that proviso is omitted in the act of 1792, and the justices moreover seem bound to allow him counsel for his defence, whose fee shall be paid by his master.‡ In case of conviction, execution of the sentence was probably very speedily performed, since the act of 1748, provides that, thereafter, it should not be performed in less than ten days, except in case of insurrection or rebellion; and further, that if the court be divided in opinion the accused should be acquitted. In 1764, an act passed, authorizing general,

* 1723. c. 4.

† 1748. c. 31.

‡ Edit. 1794. c. 103.

H 2

instead of special, commissioners of oyer and terminer,* constituting all the justices of any county, judges for the trial of slaves, committing capital offences, within their respective counties ; any four of whom, one being of the quorum, should constitute a court for that purpose: In 1772 one step further was made in favour of humanity, by an act declaring that no slave should thereafter be condemned to die unless four of the court should concur in opinion of his guilt. † The act of 1786, c. 58, confirmed by that of 1792, constitutes the justices of every county and corporation justices of oyer and terminer for the trial of slaves; ‡ requires *five* justices, at least, to constitute a court, and *unanimity* in the court for his condemnation ; allows him counsel for his defence, to be paid by his owner, and, I apprehend, admits him to object to the proceedings against him ; and finally enlarges the time of execution to *thirty* days, instead of ten (except in cases of conspiracy, insurrection, or rebellion), and extends the benefit of clergy to him in all cases, where any other person should have the benefit thereof, except in the cases before mentioned.

To an attentive observer these gradual,

*1764.
c. 9.

† 1772.
c. 9.

‡ Edit.
1794. c.
103.

and almost imperceptible amendments in our jurisprudence respecting slaves, will be found, upon the whole, of infinite importance to that unhappy race. The mode of trial in criminal cases, especially, is rendered infinitely more beneficial to them, than formerly, though perhaps still liable to exception for want of the aid of a jury: the solemnity of an oath administered the moment the trial commences, may be considered as operating more forcibly on the mind, than a general oath of office, taken, perhaps, twenty years before. Unanimity may also be more readily expected to take place among *five* men, than among *twelve*. These objections to the want of a jury are not without weight: on the other hand it may be observed, that if the number of triers be not equal to a full jury, they may yet be considered as more select; a circumstance of infinitely greater importance to the slave. The unanimity requisite in the court in order to conviction, is a more happy acquisition to the accused, than may at first appear; the opinions of the court must be delivered openly, immediately, and seriatim, beginning with the youngest judge. A single voice in favour of the accused, is an acquittal; for unanimity is not ne-

cessary, as with a jury, to acquit, as well
as to condemn: there is less danger in this
mode of trial, where the suffrages are to
be openly delivered, that a few will be
brought over to the opinion of the majority, as may too often happen among jurors, whose deliberations are in *private*,
and whose impatience of confinement may
go further than real conviction, to produce the requisite unanimity. That this
happens not unfrequently in civil cafes,
there is too much reason to believe; that
it may also happen in criminal cases,
especially where the party accused is not
one of their equals, might, not unreason-
ably, be apprehended. In New-York,
before the revolution, a slave accused of
a capital crime, should have been tried by
a jury if his master required it. This is,
perhaps, still the law of that state. Such
a provision might not be amifs in this;
but considering the ordinary run of juries
in the county-courts, I should presume
the privilege would be rarely insisted upon.

Slaves, we have seen, are now entitled
to the benefit of clergy in all cases where
it is allowed to any other offenders, except in cases of consulting, advising, or
conspiring to rebel, or make insurrection;

or plotting or conspiring to murder any person; or preparing, exhibiting, or administring medicine with an *ill* intent. The same lenity was not extended to them formerly. The act of 1748, c. 31, denied it to a slave in case of manslaughter; or the felonious breaking and entering *any* house, in the night time: or breaking and entering *any* house in the day time, and taking therefrom goods to the value of twenty shillings. The act of 1764, c. 9, extended the benefit of clergy, to a slave convicted of the manslaughter of a slave; and the act of 1772, c. 9, extended it further, to a slave convicted of house-breaking in the night time, unless such breaking be burglary; in the latter case, other offenders would be equally deprived of it. But wherever the benefit of clergy is allowed to a slave, the court, besides burning him in the hand (the usual punishment inflicted on free persons) may inflict such further corporal punishment as they may think fit; * this also seems to be the law in the case of free Negroes and mulattoes. By the act of 1723, c. 4, it was enacted, that when *any Negroe* or *mulattoe* shall be found, upon due proof made, or *pregnant circumstances*, to have given false testimony, every such offender

* 1794. c. 103.

shall, *without further trial*, have his ears successively nailed to the pillory for the space of an hour, and then cut off, and moreover receive thirty-nine lashes on his bare back, or such other punishment as the court shall think proper, not extending to life or limb. This act, with the exception of the words *pregnant circumstances*, was re-enacted in 1792. The punishment of perjury, in a *white* person, is only a fine and imprisonment. A slave convicted of hog-stealing, shall, for the first offence, receive thirty-nine lashes : any other person twenty-five : but the latter is also subject to a fine of thirty dollars, besides paying eight dollars to the owner of the hog. The punishment for the second and third offence, of this kind, is the same in the case of a free person, as of a slave; namely, by the pillory and loss of ears, for the second offence; the third is declared felony, to which clergy is, however, allowed. The preceding are the only positive distinctions which now remain between the punishment of a slave, and a white person, in those cases, where the latter is liable to a determinate corporal punishment. But we must not forget, that many actions, which are either not punishable at all, when perpe-

trated by a white perfon, or at moft, by fine
and imprifonment, only, are liable to fe-
vere corporal punifhment, when done by
a flave ; nay, even to death itfelf, in fome
cafes. To go abroad without a written
permiffion ; to keep or carry a gun, or
other weapon ; to utter any feditious
fpeech; to be prefent at any unlawful af-
fembly of flaves ; to lift the hand in op-
pofition to a white perfon, unlefs wantonly affaulted, are all offences punifhable
by whipping. * To attempt the chaftity * 1794.
of a white woman, forcibly, is punifhable c. 103.
by difmemberment : fuch an attempt
would be a high mifdemeanor in a white
free man, but the punifhment would be
far fhort of that of a flave. † To admi- † Ibidem.
nifter medicine without the order or confent of the mafter, unlefs it *appear not to
have been done with an ill intent ;* to con-
fult, advife, or confpire, to rebel or make
infurrection ; or to *confpire*, or *plot* to
murder any perfon, we have feen, are all
capital offences, from which the benefit
of clergy is utterly excluded. But a *bare
intention* to commit a felony, is not punifhable in the cafe of a free white man ;
and even the attempt, if not attended
with an actual breach of the peace, or
prevented by fuch circumftances, only,

I

as do not tend to leſſen the guilt of the offender, is at moſt a miſdemeanor by the common law : and in ſtatutable offences in general, to conſult, adviſe, and even to procure any perſon to commit a felony, does not conſtitute the crime of felony in the adviſer or procurer, unleſs the felony be actually perpetrated.

From this view of our juriſprudence reſpecting ſlaves, we are unavoidably led to remark, how frequently the laws of nature have been ſet aſide in favour of inſtitutions, the pure reſult of prejudice, uſurpation, and tyranny. We have found actions, innocent, or indifferent, puniſhable with a rigour ſcarcely due to any, but the moſt atrocious, offences againſt civil ſociety ; juſtice diſtributed by an unequal meaſure to the maſter and the ſlave ; and even the hand of mercy arreſted, where mercy might have been extended to the wretched culprit, had his complexion been the ſame with that of his judges : for, the ſhort period of ten days, between his condemnation and execution, was often inſufficient to obtain a pardon for a ſlave, convicted in a remote part of the country, whilſt a free man, condemned at the ſeat of government, and tried before the governor himſelf, in whom the power of pardoning was veſted, had a re-

spite of thirty days to implore the cle-
mency of the executive authority.—It
may be urged, and I believe with truth,
that these rigours do not proceed from a
sanguinary temper in the people of Virginia, but from those political considerations indispensibly neceffary, where slavery
prevails to any great extent : I am more-
over happy to obferve that our police re-
fpecting this unhappy class of people, is
not only less rigorous than formerly, but
perhaps milder than in any other country (r) where there are so many flaves,
or so large a proportion of them, in refpect to the free inhabitants : it is also, I
truft, unjuft to cenfure the prefent generation for the exiftence of slavery in Virginia : for I think it unqueftionably true,
that a very large proportion of our fel-
low-citizens lament that as a misfortune,
which is imputed to them as a reproach ;
it being evident from what has been already fhewn upon the fubject, that, *ante-*

(r) See Jefferfon's Notes, 259.—The Marquis de
Chatelleux's Travels, I have not noted the page ; the
Law of Retribution, by Granville Sharpe, pa. 151,
238, notes. The Juft Limitation of Slavery, by the
fame author; pa. 15, note. Ibidem, pa, 33, 50,
Ib. Append. No. 2. Encyclopédie. Tit. Efclave.
Laws of Barbadoes, &c.

cedent to the revolution; no exertion to abolish, or even to check the progress of slavery, in Virginia, could have received the smallest countenance from the crown, without whose assent the united wishes and exertions of every individual here, would have been wholly fruitless and ineffectual: it is, perhaps, also demonstrable, that at no period since the revolution, could the abolition of slavery in this state have been safely undertaken until the foundations of our newly established governments had been found capable of supporting the fabric itself, under any shock, which so arduous an attempt might have produced. But these obstacles being now happily removed, considerations of policy, as well as justice and humanity, must evince the necessity of eradicating the evil, before it becomes impossible to do it, without tearing up the roots of civil society with it.

Having in the preceding part of this enquiry shewn the origin and foundation of slavery, or the manner in which men have become slaves, as also who are liable to be retained in slavery, in Virginia, at present, with the legal consequences attendant upon their condition; it only remains to consider the mode by which

flaves have been or may be emancipated;
and the legal confequences thereof, in
this ftate.—Manumiffion, among the If-
raelites, if the bondman were an Hebrew,
was enjoined after fix years' fervice, by
the Mofaical law, unlefs the fervant chofe
to continue with his mafter, in which
cafe the mafter carried him before the
judges, and took an awl, and thruft it
through his ear into the door, * and from
thenceforth he became a fervant for ever:
but if he fent him away free, he was
bound to furnifh him liberally out of his
flock, and out of his floor, and out of his
wine-prefs. † Among the Romans, in the
time of the commonwealth, liberty could
be conferred only three ways. By tefta-
ment, by the *cenfus*, and by the *vindicta*,
or lictor's rod. A man was faid to be
free by the cenfus, " *liber cenfu*," when
his name was inferted in the cenfor's roll,
with the approbation of his mafter. When
he was freed by the vindicta, the mafter
placing his hand upon the head of the
flave, faid in the prefence of the prætor,
it is my defire that this man may be free,
" *hunc hominem liberem effe volo* ;" to
which the prætor replied, I pronounce
him free after the manner of the Romans,
" *dico cum liberum effe more quiritum.*"—

* Exod.
c. 21.
Deut. c.
15.

† Ibid.

then the lictor, receiving the *vindicta*, struck the new freed man several blows with it, upon the head, face, and back, after which his name was registered in the roll of freed-men, and his head being close shaved, a cap was given him as a token of liberty. * Under the imperial constitutions liberty might have been conferred by several other methods, as in the face of the church, in the presence of friends, or by letter, or by testament. †— But it was not in the power of every master to manumit at will; for if it were done with an intent to defraud creditors, the act was void: that is, if the master were insolvent at the time of manumission, or became insolvent by manumission, and intentionally manumitted his slave for the purpose of defrauding his creditors. A minor, under the age of twenty years, could not manumit his slave but for a just cause assigned, which must have been approved by a council, consisting of the prætor, five senators, and five knights. ‡ —In England, the mode of enfranchising villeins is said to have been thus prescribed by a law of William the Conqueror. " If any person is willing to enfranchise " his *slave*, let him, with his right hand, " deliver the slave to the sheriff in a full

* Harris's Just. in notes.

† Just. Inst. lib. 1. tit. 5. Ib. lib. 1. tit. 6.

‡ Ib. Harris's Just. in notes.

" county, proclaim him exempt from the
" bond of fervitude by manumiffion,
" fhew him open gates and ways, and
" deliver him *free arms*, to wit, a lance
" and a fword ; thereupon he is a free
" man." *—But after that period free-   * Harris's
dom was more generally conferred by   Inft. in
deed, of which Mr. Harris, in his notes   notes.
upon Juftinian, has furnifhed a prece-
dent.

In what manner manumiffion was performed in this country during the firft
century after the introduction of flavery
does not appear : the act of 1668, before
mentioned, † fhews it to have been prac-   † Ante,
tifed before that period. In 1723 an act   P. 36.
was paffed, prohibiting the manumiffion
of flaves, upon any pretence whatfoever,
except for meritorious fervices, to be
adjudged, and allowed by the governor
and council ‡. This claufe was re-enacted   ‡ 1723. c.
in 1748, and continued to be the law,   4.
until after the revolution was accom-
plifhed. The number of manumiffions
under fuch reftrictions muft neceffarily
have been very few. In May 1782 an
act paffed authorizing, generally, the manumiffion of flaves, but requiring fuch as
might be fet free, not being of found
mind or body, or being above the age of

* May
1782. c.
21.

forty-five years, or males under twenty-one, or females under eighteen, to be supported by the person liberating them, or out of his estate.* The act of manumission may be performed either by will, or by deed, under the hand and seal of the party, acknowledged by him, or proved by two witnesses in the court of the county where he resides. There is reason to believe that great numbers have been emancipated since the passing of this act. By the census of 1791 it appears that the number of free Negroes, mulattoes and Indians in Virginia, was then 12,866. It would be a large allowance, to suppose that there were 1800 free Negroes and mulattoes in Virginia when the act took effect; so that upwards of ten thousand must have been indebted to it for their freedom. (s) The number of Indians and their descendants in Virginia

(s) There are *more* free Negroes and mulattoes in Virginia alone, than are to be found in the four New-England states, and Vermont in addition to them. The progress of emancipation in this state is therefore much greater than our *Eastern* brethren may at first suppose. There are only 1087 free Negroes and mulattoes in the States of New-York, New-Jersey and Pennsylvania, *more*, than in Virginia. Those who take a subject in the gross, have little idea of the result of an exact scrutiny. Out of 20,348 inhabitants on

at present, is too small to require particular notice. The progress of emancipation in Virginia, is at this time continual, but not rapid; a second census will enable us to form a better judgment of it than at present. The act passed in 1792 accords in some degree with the Justinian code, * by providing that slaves emancipated may be taken in execution to satisfy any debt contracted by the person emancipating them, before such emancipation is made. (t)

* 1794. c. 103.

the Eastern Shore of Virginia 1185 were free Negroes and mulattoes when the census was taken. The number is since much augmented.

(t) The act of 1795. c. 11. enacts, that any person held in slavery may make complaint to a magistrate, or to the court of the district county or corporation wherein he resides, and not elsewhere. The magistrate, if the complaint be made to him, shall issue his warrant to summon the owner before him, and compel him to give bond and security to suffer the complainant to appear at the next court to petition the court to be admitted to sue *in formâ pauperis*. If the owner refuse, the magistrate shall order the complainant into the custody of the officer serving the warrant, at the expence of the master, who shall keep him until the sitting of the court, and then produce him before it. Upon petition to the court, if the court be satisfied as to the material facts, they shall assign the complainant council, who shall state the facts with his opinion thereon to the court; and unless from the circumstances so

Among the Romans, the *libertini*, or freedmen, were formerly diſtinguiſhed by a threefold diviſion. * They ſometimes obtained what was called the greater liberty, thereby becoming *Roman citizens*. To this privilege, thoſe who were enfranchiſed by teſtament, by the cenſus, or by the vindicta, appear to have been alone admitted: ſometimes they obtained the leſſer liberty only, and became *Latins ;* whoſe condition is thus deſcribed by Juſtinian. " They never enjoyed the right " of ſucceſſion [to eſtates].—For al- " though they led the lives of free men, " yet with their laſt breath they loſt both " their lives and liberties ; for their poſ- " ſeſſions, like the goods of ſlaves, were " detained by the manumittor." † Sometimes they obtained only the inferior liber-

ſtated, and the opinion thereon given, the court ſhall *ſee manifeſt reaſon to deny their interference,* they ſhall order the clerk to iſſue proceſs againſt the owner, and the complainant ſhall remain in the cuſtody of the ſheriff until the owner ſhall give bond and ſecurity to have him forthcoming to anſwer the judgment of the court. And by the general law in caſe of pauper's ſuits, the complainants ſhall have writs of ſubpœna gratis ; and by the practice of the courts, he is permitted to attend the taking the depoſitions of witneſſes, and go and come freely to and from court, for the proſecution of his ſuit.

ty, being called *dedititii:* such were slaves who had been condemned as criminals, and afterwards obtained manumission through the indulgence of their masters: their conditions was equalled with that of conquered revolters, whom the Romans called, in reproach, *dedititii, quia se suaque omnia dediderunt:* but all these distinctions were abolished by Justinian, * by whom all freed men in general were made citizens of Rome, without regard to the form of manumission.—In England, the presenting the villein with *free arms,* seems to have been the symbol of his restoration to all the rights which a feudatory was entitled to. With us, we have seen that emancipation does not confer the rights of citizenship on the person emancipated; on the contrary, both he and his posterity, of the same complexion with himself, must always labour under many civil incapacities. If he is absolved from personal restraint, or corporal punishment, by a master, yet the laws restrain his actions in many instances, where there is none upon a free white man. If he can maintain a suit, he cannot be a witness, a juror, or a judge in any controversy between one of his own complexion and a white person. If he can

* Inst. lib. 1. tit. 5. f. 3.

K 2

acquire property in lands, he cannot exercise the right of suffrage, which such a
property would confer on his former mafter ; much lefs can he affift in making
thofe laws by which he is bound. Yet,
even under thefe difabilities, his prefent
condition bears an enviable pre-eminence
over his former ftate. Poffeffing the liberty of loco-motion, which was formerly
denied him, it is in his choice to fubmit
to that civil inferiority, infeparably attached to his condition in this country,
or feek fome more favourable climate,
where all diftinctions between men are
either totally abolifhed, or lefs regarded
than in this.

The extirpation of flavery from the
United States, is a tafk equally arduous
and momentous. To reftore the bleffings
of liberty to near a million *(u)* of op-
preffed individuals, who have groaned
under the yoke of bondage, and to their
defcendants, is an object, which thofe
who truft in Providence, will be convinced would not be unaided by the di-
vine Author of our being, fhould we in-
voke his bleffing upon our endeavours.

(u) The number of flaves in the United States at
the time of the late cenfus, was fomething under
700,000.

Yet human prudence forbids that we
should precipitately engage in a work of
such hazard as a general and simultaneous
emancipation. The mind of man must
in some measure be formed for his future
condition. The early impressions of obe-
dience and submission, which slaves have
received among us, and the no less habi-
tual arrogance and assumption of superi-
ority, among the whites, contribute, e-
qually, to unfit the former for *freedom*,
and the latter for *equality*. *(v)* To expel

(v) Mr. Jefferson most forcibly paints the unhappy
influence on the manners of the people produced by
the existence of slavery among us. The whole commerce between master and slave, says he, is a perpetual
exercise of the most boisterous passions, the most
unremitting despotism on the one part, and degrad-
ing submissions on the other. Our children see
this, and learn to imitate it ; for man is an imitative
animal. This quality is the germ of education in him.
From his cradle to his grave he is learning what he sees
others do. If a parent had no other motive either in
his own philanthropy or his self-love, for restraining
the intemperance of passion towards his slave, it should
always be a sufficient one that his child is present. But
generally it is not sufficient. The parent storms, the
child looks on, catches the lineaments of wrath, puts
on the same airs in the circle of smaller slaves, gives a
loose to his worst of passions ; and thus nursed, edu-
cated, and daily exercised in tyranny, cannot but be
stamped by it with odious peculiarities. The man

them all at once, from the United States,
would in fact be to devote them only to

muſt be a prodigy who can retain his manners and
morals undepraved by ſuch circumſtances. And with
what execrations would the ſtateſman be loaded, who
permitting one half the citizens thus to trample on the
rights of the other, transforms them into deſpots, and
theſe into enemies, deſtroys the morals of the one part,
and the amor patriæ of the other. For if a ſlave can
have a country in this world, it muſt be any other in
preference to that in which he is born to live and labour for another: in which he muſt lock up the faculties of his nature, contribute as far as depends on his
individual endeavours to the evaniſhment of the human
race, or entail his own miſerable condition on the end-
leſs generations proceeding from him. With the morals of the people, their induſtry alſo, is deſtroyed.
For in a warm climate, no man will labour for himſelf
who can make another labour for him. This is ſo
true, that of the proprietors of ſlaves a very ſmall proportion indeed are ever ſeen to labour. And can the
liberties of a nation be ever thought ſecure when we
have removed their only firm baſis, a conviction in the
minds of the people, that theſe liberties are of the gift
of God? That they are not to be violated but with
his wrath? Indeed I tremble for my country when
I reflect that God is juſt: that his juſtice cannot ſleep
for ever: that conſidering numbers, nature, and natural means only, a revolution of the wheel of fortune,
an exchange of ſituation is among poſſible events: that
it may become probable by ſupernatural interference!
The Almighty has no attribute which can take ſide
with us in ſuch a conteſt.—But it is impoſſible to be
temperate and to purſue this ſubject through the va-

a lingering death by famine, by difease, and other accumulated miferies : " We " have in hiftory but one picture of a fi- " milar enterprize, and there we fee it " was neceffary not only to open the fea " by a miracle, for them to pafs, but more " neceffary to clofe it again to prevent " their return. * To retain them among us, would be nothing more than to throw fo many of the human race upon the earth without the means of fubfiftence: they would foon become idle, profligate, and miferable. Unfit for their new con- dition, and unwilling to return to their former laborious courfe, they would be- come the caterpillars of the earth, and the tigers of the human race. The recent hiftory of the French Weft Indies exhibits a melancholy picture of the probable con- fequences of a general, and momentary

* Letter from Jas. Sullivan, Efq. to Dr. Bel- knap.

rious confiderations of policy, of morals, of hiftory, natural and civil. We muft be contented to hope they will force their way into every one's mind. I think a change already perceptible, fince the origin of the prefent revolution. The fpirit of the mafter is abating, that of the flave rifing from the duft ; his condition mollifying ; the way I hope preparing, un- der the aufpices of Heaven, for a total emancipation, and that this is difpofed in the order of events, to be with the confent of their mafters, rather than by their extirpation. Notes on Virginia, 298.

emancipation in any of the states, where slavery has made considerable progress. In Massachusetts the abolition of it was effected by a single stroke ; a clause in their constitution : * but the whites at that time, were as sixty-five to one, in proportion to the blacks. The whole number of free persons in the United States, south of Delaware state, are 1,233,829, and there are 648,439 slaves ; the proportion being less than two to one. Of the cultivators of the earth in the same district, it is probable that there are four slaves for one free white man.——To discharge the former from their present condition, would be attended with an immediate general famine, in those parts of the United States, from which not all the productions of the other states, could deliver them ; similar evils might reasonably be apprehended from the adoption of the measure by any one of the southern states ; for in all of them the proportion of slaves is too great, not to be attended with calamitous effects, if they were immediately set free. (w) These are serious, I had

* Dr. Belkkap.

(w) What is here advanced is not to be understood as implying an opinion that the labour of slaves is more productive than that of freemen.—The author of the Treatise on the Wealth of Nations, informs us, " That

almost said unsurmountable obstacles, to
a general, simultaneous emancipation.—
There are other considerations not to be
disregarded. A great part of the *property*
of individuals consists in *slaves*. The
laws have sanctioned this species of property. Can the laws take away the property of an individual without his own
consent, or without a *just compensation*?
Will those who do not hold slaves agree
to be taxed to make this compensation?
Creditors also, who have trusted their
debtors upon the faith of this visible property will be defrauded. If justice de-
mands the emancipation of the slave, she
also, *under these circumstances*, seems to
plead for the owner, and for his creditor.
The claims of nature, it will be said are
stronger than those which arise from so-
cial institutions, only. I admit it, but
nature also dictates to us to provide for
our *own* safety, and authorizes all *necessary*

" it appears from the experience of all ages and na-
" tions, that the work done by freemen comes cheaper
" in the end than that done by slaves. That it is
" found to do so, even in Boston, New-York and
" Philadelphia, where the wages of common labour are
" very high." Vol. 1. pa. 123. Lond. edit. oct.
Admitting this conclusion, it would not remove the
objection that emancipated slaves would not willingly
labour.

L

measures for that purpose. And we have
shewn that our own security, nay, our
very existence, might be endangered by
the hasty adoption of any measure for the
immediate relief of the *whole* of this unhappy race. Must we then quit the subject, in despair of the success of any pro-
ject for the amendment of their, as well
as our own, condition? I think not.—
Strenuously as I feel my mind opposed to
a simultaneous emancipation, for the reasons already mentioned, the abolition
of slavery in the United States, and especially in that state, to which I am attached
by every tie that nature and society form,
is *now* my *first*, and will probably be my
last, expiring wish. But here let me
avoid the imputation of inconsistency, by
observing, that the abolition of slavery
may be effected without the *emancipation*
of a single slave; without depriving any
man of the *property* which he *possesses*,
and without defrauding a creditor who
has trusted him on the faith of that property. The experiment in that mode
has already been begun in some of our
sister states. Pennsylvania, under the
auspices of the immortal Franklin, (x)

(x) Doctor Franklin, it is said, drew the bill for
the gradual abolition of slavery in Pennsylvania.

begun the work of gradual abolition of
flavery in the year 1780, by enlisting nature herself, on the side of humanity.
Connecticut followed the example four
years after. (y) New-York very lately
made an essay which miscarried, by a very
inconsiderable majority. Mr. Jefferson informs us, that the committee of revisors,
of which he was a member, had prepared
a bill for the emancipation of all slaves
born after passing that act. This is conformable to the Pennsylvania and Connecticut laws.—Why the measure was
not brought forward in the general assembly I have never heard. Possibly be-
cause objections were foreseen to that
part of the bill which relates to the disposal of the blacks, after they had attained
a certain age. (z) It certainly seems li-

(y) It is probable that similar laws have been passed
in some other states; but I have not been able to procure a note of them.

(z) The object of the amendment proposed to be
offered to the legislature, was to emancipate all slaves
born after a certain period; and further directing that
they should continue with their parents to a certain
age, then be brought up, at the public expence, to
tillage, arts, or sciences, according to their geniuses,
till the females should be eighteen, and the males
twenty-one years of age, when they should be colonized
to such a place as the circumstances of the time should

-able to many, both as to the policy and the practicability of it. To establish such a colony in the territory of the United States, would probably lay the foundation of inteſtine wars, which would terminate only in their extirpation, or final expulſion. To attempt it in any other quarter of the globe would be attended with the utmoſt cruelty to the colonists, themſelves, and the deſtruction of their whole race. If the plan were at this moment in operation, it would require the annual exportation of 12,000 perſons. This requiſite number muſt, for a ſeries of years be conſiderably increaſed, in order to keep pace with the increaſing population of thoſe people. In twenty years it would amount to upwards of twenty thouſand perſons; which is half the number which are now ſuppoſed to be annually

-iender moſt proper; ſending them out with arms, implements of houſehold and of the handicraft arts, ſeeds, pairs of the uſeful domeſtic animals, &c. to declare them a free and independent people, and extend to them our alliance and protection, till they ſhall have acquired ſtrength; and to ſend veſſels at the ſame time to other parts of the world for an equal number of white inhabitants; to induce whom to migrate hither, proper encouragements ſhould be propoſed. Notes on Virginia, 251.

exported from Africa.—Where would a fund to support this expence be found? Five times the present revenue of the state would barely defray the charge of their passage. Where provisions for their support after their arrival? Where those necessaries which must preserve them from perishing?—Where a territory sufficient to support them?—Or where could they be received as friends, and not as invaders? To colonize them in the United States might seem less difficult. If the territory to be assigned them were beyond the settlements of the whites, would they not be put upon a forlorn hope against the Indians? Would not the expence of transporting them thither, and supporting them, at least for the first and second year, be also far beyond the revenues and abilities of the state? The expence attending a small army in that country hath been found enormous. To transport as many colonists, annually, as we have shewn were necessary to eradicate the evil, would probably require five times as much money as the support of such an army. But the expence would not stop there: they must be assisted and supported at least for another year after their arrival in their new settlements. Suppose them arrived. Illiterate and ignorant as they are, is it probable that they would be capable of inftituting fuch a government, in their new colony, as would be neceffary for their own internal happinefs, or to fecure them from deftruction from without? European emigrants, from whatever country they arrive, have been accuftomed to the reftraint of laws, and to refpect for government. Thefe people, accuftomed to be ruled with a rod of iron, will not eafily fubmit to milder reftraints. They would become hordes of vagabonds, robbers and murderers. Without the aids of an enlightened policy, morality, or religion, what elfe could be expected from their ftill favage ftate, and debafed condition?—" But why not retain and " *incorporate the blacks into the ftate?*" This queftion has been well anfwered by Mr. Jefferfon, *(a)* and who is there fo

---

(a) It will probably be afked, why not retain the blacks among us and *incorporate them into the ftate?* Deep-rooted prejudices entertained by the whites; ten thoufand recollections by the blacks, of the injuries they have fuftained; new provocations; the *real diftinctions* which *nature* has made; and many other circumftances will divide us into parties and produce convulfions, which will probably never end but in the extermination of one or the other race. To thefe objections which are political may be added others which are

free from prejudices among us, as candidly to declare that he has none against

physical and moral. The first difference which strikes us is that of colour.—&c. The circumstance of superior beauty is thought worthy attention in the propagation of our horses, dogs, and other domestic animals; why not in that of man? &c. In general their existence appears to participate more of sensation than reflection. Comparing them by their faculties of memory, reason and imagination, it appears to me that in memory they are equal to the whites; in reason much inferior; that in imagination they are dull, tasteless and anamolous. &c. The improvement of the blacks in body and mind, in the first instance of their mixture with the whites, has been observed by every one, and proves that their inferiority is not the effect merely of their condition of life. We know that among the Romans, about the Augustan age, especially, the condition of their slaves was much more deplorable, than that of the blacks on the continent of America. Yet among the Romans their slaves were often their rarest artists. They excelled too in science, insomuch as to be usually employed as tutors to their masters' children. Epictetus, Terence, and Phædrus were slaves. But they were of the race of whites. It is not their condition then, but nature, which has produced the distinction. The opinion that they are inferior in the faculties of reason and imagination, must be hazarded with great diffidence. To justify a general conclusion requires many observations. &c.—I advance it therefore as a suspicion only, that the blacks, whether originally a distinct race, or made distinct by time and circumstances, are inferior to the whites both in the endowments of body and mind. &c. This unsuch a measure? The recent scenes transacted in the French colonies in the West Indies are enough to make one shudder with the apprehension of realizing similar calamities in this country. Such probably would be the event of an attempt to smother those prejudices which have been cherished for a period of almost two centuries. Those who secretly favour, whilst they affect to regret, domestic slavery, contend that in abolishing it, we must also abolish that scion from it which I have denominated *civil* slavery. That there must be no distinction of rights; that the descendants of Africans, as men, have an equal claim to all civil rights, as the descendants of Europeans; and upon being delivered from the yoke of bondage have

fortunate difference of colour, and perhaps of faculty, is a powerful obstacle to the emancipation of these people. Among the Romans emancipation required but one effort. The slave, when made free, might mix with, without staining, the blood of his master. But with us a second is necessary, unknown to history. —See the passage at length, Notes on Virginia, page 252 to 265.

" In the present case, it is not only the slave who " is beneath his master, it is the Negroe who is be- " neath the white man. No act of enfranchisement " can efface this unfortunate distinction." Chatelleux's Travels in America.

a right to be admitted to all the privileges
of a citizen.—But have not men when
they enter into a state of society, a right
to admit, or exclude any description of
persons, as they think proper? If it be
true, as Mr. Jefferson seems to suppose,
that the Africans are really an inferior
race of mankind, (b) will not sound policy advise their exclusion from a society
in which they have not yet been admitted
to participate in civil rights; and even to
guard against such admission, at any future
period, since it may eventually depreciate
the whole national character? And if
prejudices have taken such deep root in
our minds, as to render it impossible to
eradicate this opinion, ought not so general an error, if it be one, to be respect-
ed? Shall we not relieve the necessities
of the naked diseased beggar, unless we
will invite him to a seat at our table; nor
afford him shelter from the inclemencies
of the night air, unless we admit him also

(b) The celebrated David Hume, in his Essay on
National Character, advances the same opinion; Doctor Beattie, in his Essay on Truth, controverts it with
many powerful arguments. Early prejudices, had we
more satisfactory information than we can possibly possess on the subject at present, would render an inha-
bitant of a country where Negroe slavery prevails, an
improper umpire between them.

M

to fhare our bed ? To deny that we ought
to abolifh flavery, without incorporating
the Negroes into the ftate, and admitting
them to a full participation of all our
civil and focial rights, appears to me to
reft upon a fimilar foundation. The experiment fo far as it has been already
made among us, proves that the emancipated blacks are not ambitious of civil
rights. To prevent the generation of
fuch an ambition, appears to comport
with found policy ; for if it fhould ever
rear its head, its partizans, as well as its
opponents, will be enlifted by nature her-
felf, and always ranged in formidable
array againft each other. We muft therefore endeavour to find fome middle courfe,
between the tyrannical and iniquitous policy which holds fo many human creatures
in a ftate of grievous bondage, and that
which would turn loofe a numerous,
ftarving, and enraged banditti, upon the
innocent defcendants of their former op-
preffors. *Nature, time,* and *found policy*
muft co-operate with each other to produce fuch a change : if either be neglected, the work will be incomplete, dan-
gerous, and not improbably deftructive.
The plan therefore which I would prefume to propofe for the confideration of my

countrymen is such, as the number of slaves, the difference of their nature, and habits, and the state of agriculture, among us, might render it *expedient*, rather than *desirable* to adopt: and would partake partly of that proposed by Mr. Jefferson, and adopted in other states; and partly of such cautionary restrictions, as a due regard to situation and circumstances, and even to *general* prejudices, might recommend to those, who engage in so arduous, and perhaps unprecedented an undertaking.

1. Let every female born after the adoption of the plan be free, and transmit freedom to all her descendants, both male and female.

2. As a compensation to those persons, in whose families such females, or their descendants may be born, for the expence and trouble of their maintenance during infancy, let them serve such persons until the age of twenty-eight years: let them then receive twenty dollars in money, two suits of clothes, suited to the season, a hat, a pair of shoes, and two blankets. If these things be not voluntarily done, let the county courts enforce the performance, upon complaint.

3. Let all Negroe children be registered with the clerk of the county or corpora-

tion court, where born, within one month after their birth : let the person in whose family they are born take a copy of the register, and deliver it to the mother, or if she die to the child, before it is of the age of twenty-one years. Let any Negroe claiming to be free, and above the age of puberty, be considered as of the age of twenty-eight years, if he or she be not registered, as required.

4. Let all such Negroe servants be put on the same footing as white servants and apprentices now are, in respect to food, raiment, correction, and the assignment of their service from one to another.

5. Let the children of Negroes and mulattoes, born in the families of their parents, be bound to service by the overseers of the poor, until they shall attain the age of twenty-one years.—Let all above that age, who are not housekeepers, nor have voluntarily bound themselves to service for a year before the first day of February annually, be then bound for the remainder of the year by the overseers of the poor. Let the overseers of the poor receive fifteen per cent. of their wages, from the person hiring them, as a compensation for their trouble, and ten per cent. per annum out of the wa-

ges of such as they may bind apprentices.

6. If at the age of twenty-seven years,
the master of a Negroe or mulattoe servant be unwilling to pay his freedom
dues, above mentioned, at the expiration
of the succeeding year, let him bring him
into the county court, clad and furnished
with necessaries as before directed, and pay
into court five dollars, for the use of the
servant, and thereupon let the court di-
rect him to be hired by the overseers of
the poor for the succeeding year, in the
manner before directed.

7. Let no Negroe or mulattoe be capable
of taking, holding, or exercising, any public office, freehold, franchise or privilege,
or any estate in lands or tenements, other
than a lease not exceeding twenty-one
years.—Nor of keeping, or bearing arms,
(c) unless authorifed so to do by some
act of the general assembly, whose duration shall be limitted to three years. Nor
of contracting matrimony with any other
than a Negroe or mulattoe ; nor be an at-
torney ; nor be a juror ; nor a witness in
any court of judicature, except against,

(c) See Spirit of Laws, 12—15.——1. Black
Com. 417.

or between Negroes and mulattoes. Nor be an executor or administrator; nor capable of making any will or testament; nor maintain any real action; nor be a trustee of lands or tenements himself, nor any other person to be a trustee to him or to his use.

8. Let all persons born after the passing of the act, be considered as entitled to the same mode of trial in criminal cases, as free Negroes and mulattoes are now entitled to.

The restrictions in this place may appear to favour strongly of prejudice: whoever proposes any plan for the abolition of slavery, will find that he must either encounter, or accommodate himself to prejudice.—I have preferred the latter; not that I pretend to be wholly exempt from it, but that I might avoid as many obstacles as possible to the completion of so desirable a work, as the abolition of slavery. Though I am opposed to the banishment of the Negroes, I wish not to encourage their future residence among us. By denying them the most valuable privileges which civil government affords, I wished to render it their inclination and their interest to seek those privileges in some other climate. There

is an immense unsettled territory on this
continent *(d)* more congenial to their
natural conftitutions than ours, where
they may perhaps be received upon more
favourable terms than we can permit
them to remain with us. Emigrating in
fmall numbers, they will be able to effect
fettlements more eafily than in large numbers ; and without the expence or danger
of numerous colonies. By releafing them
from the yoke of bondage, and enabling
them to feek happinefs wherever they can
hope to find it, we furely confer a benefit, which no one can fufficiently appreciate, who has not tafted of the bitter
curfe of compulfory fervitude. By ex-
cludidg them from offices, the feeds of
ambition would be buried too deep, ever
to germinate : by difarming them, we
may calm our apprehenfions of their re-
fentments arifing from paft fufferings ; by

(d) The immenfe territory of Louifiana, which extends as far fouth as the lat. 25° and the two Floridas,
would probably afford a ready afylum for fuch as might
choofe to become Spanifh fubjects. How far their political rights might be enlarged in thefe countries, is,
however queftionable : but the climate is undoubtedly
more favourable to the African conftitution than ours,
and from this caufe, it is not improbable that emigra-
tions from thefe ftates would in time be very confidera-
ble.

incapacitating them from holding lands, we should add one inducement more to emigration, and effectually remove the foundation of ambition, and party-struggles. Their personal rights, and their property, though limited, would whilst they remain among us be under the protection of the laws; and their condition not at all inferior to that of the *labouring* poor in most other countries. Under such an arrangement we might reasonably hope, that time would either remove from us a race of men, whom we wish not to incorporate with us, or obliterate those prejudices, which now form an obstacle to such incorporation.

But it is not from the want of liberality to the emancipated race of blacks that I apprehend the most serious objections to the plan I have ventured to suggest.— Those slave holders (whose numbers I trust are few) who have been in the habit of considering their fellow creatures as no more than cattle, and the rest of the brute creation, will exclaim that they are to be deprived of their *property*, without compensation. Men who will shut their ears against this moral truth, that all men are by nature *free*, and *equal*, will not even be convinced that they do not

poſſeſs a *property* in an *unborn* child : they
will not diſtinguiſh between allowing to
unborn generations the abſolute and una-
lienable rights of human nature, and taking away that which they *now poſſeſs* ;
they will ſhut their ears againſt truth,
ſhould you tell them, the loſs of the mother's labour for nine months, and the
maintenance of a child for a dozen or
fourteen years, is amply compenſated by
the ſervices of that child for as many
years more, as he has been an expence to
them. But if the voice of reaſon, juſtice
and humanity be not ſtifled by ſordid avarice, or unfeeling tyranny, it would be
eaſy to convince even thoſe who have entertained ſuch erroneous notions, that the
right of one man over another is neither
founded in nature, nor in ſound policy.
That it cannot extend to thoſe *not in being ;* that no man can in reality be *deprived*
of what he doth not poſſeſs : that fourteen
years labour by a young perſon in the
prime of life, is an ample compenſation
for a few months of labour loſt by the
mother, and for the maintenance of a
child, in that coarſe homely manner that
Negroes are brought up : And laſtly, that
a ſtate of ſlavery is not only perfectly incompatible with the principles of govern-

N

ment, but with the safety and security of their masters. History evinces this. At this moment we have the most awful demonstrations of it. Shall we then neglect a duty, which every consideration, moral, religious, political, or *selfish*, recommends. Those who wish to postpone the measure, do not reflect that every day renders the task more arduous to be performed. We have now 300,000 slaves among us. Thirty years hence we shall have double the number. In sixty years we shall have 1,200,000. And in less than another century from this day, even that enormous number will be doubled. Milo acquired strength enough to carry an ox, by beginning with the ox while he was yet a calf. If we complain that the calf is too heavy for our shoulders, what will not the ox be?

To such as apprehend danger to our agricultural interest, and the depriving the families of those whose principal reliance is upon their slaves, of support, it will be proper to submit a view of the gradual operation, and effects of this plan. They will no doubt be surprized to hear, that whenever it is adopted, the number of slaves will not be diminished for forty years after it takes place; that it will even encrease for thirty years; that at the diſtance of ſixty years, there will be one-third of the number at its firſt commencement : that it will require *above a century* to complete it ; and that the number of blacks *under twenty-eight*, and conſequently bound to ſervice, in the families they are born in, will always be at leaſt as great, as the preſent number of ſlaves. Theſe circumſtances I truſt will remove many objections, and that they are truly ſtated will appear upon enquiry. *(e)* It

(e) As it may not be unacceptable to ſome readers to obſerve the operation of this plan, I ſhall ſubjoin the following ſtatement :

PRELIMINARY REMARKS.

1. The number of ſlaves in Virginia by the late cenſus being found to be 292,427, they may now, in round numbers be eſtimated at   300,000

2. Let it be ſuppoſed that the males and females are nearly or altogether equal in number.

3. According to Dr. Franklin, the people of America double their numbers in about twenty-eight years ; and according to Mr. Jefferſon, the negroes increaſe as faſt as the whites, they will therefore double, at leaſt every thirty years.

4. Let it be ſuppoſed that in thirty years one half of the preſent race of negroes will be extinct.

5. Let it be ſuppoſed that in forty-five years there will not remain more than one-fifth of the preſent race alive.

will further appear, that females only
will arrive at the age of emancipation
within the first forty-five years; all the
males during that period, continuing either in flavery, or bound to fervice, till

6. Let it be likewife fuppofed, that in
fixty years the whole of the prefent race will
be extinct.

7. For concifenefs fake, let the prefent
race be called *ante-nati*, thofe born after the
adoption of the plan, *poft-nati*.

FROM HENCE IT WILL FOLLOW,

1. That the prefent number of flaves being 300,000

2. In thirty years their numbers will
amount to   -   -   -   600,000

3. But at that period as one half of them
will be extinct, (rem. 4.) their numbers
will ftand thus:

Ante-nati, - 150,000
Poft-nati, - 450,000
——————— 600,000

4. The mean increafe of the poft-nati
for the next thirty years will therefore be
$\frac{450000}{30}$, annually, or   -   -   15,000

5. If one half of thefe be males, who are
ftill to remain flaves, there will in the firft
fixteen years, be born   -   -   120,000

6. After the firft fixteen years, the poft-
nati females will begin to breed; the proportion of males born to flavery in the next
twelve years may be eftimated at one-fourth
of the whole number born after the commencement of that period. Their number
will be   -   -   -   52,000

the age of twenty-eight years. The earth, cannot want cultivators, whilst our population increases as at present, and three-fourths of those employed therein are held to service, and the remainder compella-

7. The number of *slaves* living in Virginia at the end of *thirty* years from the adoption of the plan, will be, ante-nati (prop. 3.) - - - 150,000
Post-nati males born in the first
 16 years, - - - 120,000
Post-nati males born in the last
 12 years, - - - 52,500
        ——— 322,500

8. The number of *negroes* at the same time will stand thus:
   Slaves, - - - 322,500
   Post-nati free born, 277,500
        ——— 600,000

9. After twenty-eight years from the first adoption, this plan of gradual emancipation will first begin to manifest its effects, by the complete emancipation of one twenty-eighth part of the post-nati free born during that period each succeeding year, for twenty-eight years more; their numbers will be, $\frac{277500}{28}$, or - - - 9,910
These will be all females.

10. It being admitted that the negroes double every thirty years, the supposition that in forty-five years, their numbers will be half as many more as in thirty, will not be very erroneous, if so, the whole race of them at that period will be - - 900,000

ble to labour. For we muſt not loſe ſight of this important conſideration, that theſe people muſt be *bound* to labour, if they

11. Their numbers will ſtand thus :

Ante-nati,	-	60,000
Poſt-nati,	-	840,000
		900,000

12. After twenty-eight years are paſt, the number of ſlaves born muſt continually diminiſh. Suppoſe their number born in the laſt 17 years, to be one-fourth as many as thoſe born in the preceding twelve years, they will be $\frac{52400}{4}$, or - 13,125

13. The ſlaves in Virginia in forty-five years will then be, ante-nati, - 60,000

Poſt-nati males born in the firſt
sixteen years, - - - 120,000
Ditto, born in the next twelve
years, - - - 52,500
Ditto, born in the laſt seventeen years, - - - 13,125
245,625

At this period the emancipation of males will begin.

14. But after twenty-eight years it has been ſhewn that 9,910 negroes will annually arrive at the age of emancipation, their whole number in forty-five years will be 168,470

15. The ſtate of the negroes at the end of 45 years, will then be, ſlaves, - 245,625
Poſt-nati fully emancipated (females), - - - 168,470
Poſt-nati not emancipated, - 485,905
900,000

do not *voluntarily* engage therein. Their faculties are at present only calculated for that object ; if they be not employed

16. In fixty years the whole number of negroes will be -   -   -   -   1,200,000

17. At that period the whole of the present race will be extinct ; and we may also infer that one half of those born in the first thirty years will be also extinct ; the number of slaves born in that period has been shewn, (prop. 7.) to be 172,500, the number of these then living will be ¹⁷²⁵⁰⁰, or   -   86,250

18. One half of the post-nati free born, during that period, being now fully emancipated, may be likewise presumed to be extinct ; their numbers (prop. 8.) will be, ¹⁷²⁵⁰⁰, or -   -   -   -   138,750

19. The state of the negroes at the end of fixty years, will therefore be :

Slaves born during the first thirty years, - -	86,250
Ditto born after that period, -	13,125
Post-nati fully emancipated, -	138,750
Post-nati under 28 years of age,	961,875
	————1,200,000

20. At the end of ninety years the number of negroes will be -   -   -   2,400,000

21. Of this number, those only born after the first thirty years, being supposed to be living, the number of slaves (prop. 12) will then be reduced to -   -   -   13,125

22. And as the last mentioned number of slaves are supposed to be born within forty-five years, their whole number will be extinct

therein they will become drones of the worft. defcription. In abfolving them from the yoke of flavery, we muft not forget the interefts of the fociety. Thofe interefts require the exertions of every individual in fome mode or other ; and thofe who have not wherewith to fupport themfelves honeftly without corporal la- bour, whatever be their complexion, ought to be compelled to labour. This is the cafe in England, where domeftic flavery has long been unknown. It muft alfo be the cafe in every well ordered fo- ciety ; and where the numbers of perfons without property increafe, there the co- ertion of the laws becomes more immedi- ately requifite. The propofed plan would neceffarily have this effect, and therefore ought to be accompanied with fuch a re- gulation. Though the rigours of our po- lice in refpect to this unhappy race ought

in fifteen years more, that is, in *one hundred* and *five* years from the firft adoption of the plan.

23. By prop. 19. it appears, that out of 1,200,000 negroes, there will then be 961,875 under the age of twenty-eight years, the period of emancipation.

24. We may therefore conclude, that from *two-thirds* to *three-fourths* of the whole num- ber of blacks will *always* be liable to fervice.

to be softened, yet, its regularity, and punctual administration should be increased, rather than relaxed. If we doubt the propriety of such measures, what must we think of the situation of our country, when instead of 300,000, we shall have more than *two millions* of SLAVES among us? This *must happen within a* CENTURY, if we do not set about the abolition of slavery. Will not our posterity curse the days of their nativity with all the anguish of Job? Will they not execrate the memory of those ancestors, who, having it in their power to avert evil, have, like their first parents, entailed a curse upon all future generations? We know that the rigour of the laws respecting slaves unavoidably must increase with their numbers: What a blood-stained code must that be which is calculated for the restraint of *millions* held in bondage! Such must our unhappy country exhibit within a century, unless we are both wise and just enough to avert from posterity the calamity and reproach, which are otherwise unavoidable.

I am not vain enough to presume the plan I have suggested entirely free from objection; nor that in offering my own ideas on the subject, I have been more for-

tunate than others: but from the commu-
nication of fentiment between thofe who
lament the evil, it is poffible that an ef-
fectual remedy may at length be difco-
vered. Whenever that happens the golden
age of our country will begin. Till then,

———————*Non hofpes ab hofpite tutus,*
Non Herus à Famulo: fratrum quoque gratia rara.

THE END.

CPSIA information can be obtained
at www.ICGtesting.com
Printed in the USA
BVOW06*2047281117
501496BV00004B/34/P